GOD'S HALL of FAITH
Hebrews 11
Devotional Commentary

Dr. Larry Petton

2017

Elm Springs, Arkansas

BOOKS by Dr. Larry Petton

The Cancer of Unforgiveness

Daddy, What Does It Feel Like to Die?

God, Why Is This Happening To America?
(Devotional Commentary on Habakkuk)

When Lucifer Left Heaven

Valleys
(Psalm 23)

John 15
Self-Study Guide

God's Hall of Faith
(Hebrews 11 Devotional Commentary)

ODIE

Greatest Dog Ever
Greatest Friend Ever
You taught me how to be a Shepherd.
I will never forget you.

Trust
in the Lord with all your heart
and lean not on your own understanding;
in all your ways submit to him,
and he will make your paths straight.

Proverbs 3:5-6

Let's Go On A Journey Together!

Read one verse in Hebrews chapter 11 each day for 40 days.

Read the daily devotional and answer the personal questions.

Keep this book for a personal journal of your journey with Jesus.

Hebrews 11

1 Now faith is confidence in what we hope for and assurance about what we do not see. 2 This is what the ancients were commended for.

3 By faith we understand that the universe was formed at God's command, so that what is seen was not made out of what was visible.

4 By faith Abel brought God a better offering than Cain did. By faith he was commended as righteous, when God spoke well of his offerings. And by faith Abel still speaks, even though he is dead.

5 By faith Enoch was taken from this life, so that he did not experience death: "He could not be found, because God had taken him away." For before he was taken, he was commended as one who pleased God. 6 And without faith it is impossible to please God, because anyone who comes to him must believe that he exists and that he rewards those who earnestly seek him.

7 By faith Noah, when warned about things not yet seen, in holy fear built an ark to save his family. By his faith he condemned the world and became heir of the righteousness that is in keeping with faith.

8 By faith Abraham, when called to go to a place he would later receive as his inheritance, obeyed and went, even though he did not know where he was going. 9 By faith he made his home in the promised land like a stranger in a foreign country; he lived in tents, as did Isaac and Jacob, who were heirs with him of the same promise. 10 For he was looking forward to the city with foundations, whose architect and builder is God. 11 And by faith even Sarah, who was past childbearing age, was enabled to bear children because she considered him faithful who had made the promise. 12 And so from this one man, and he as good as dead, came descendants as numerous as the stars in the sky and as countless as the sand on the seashore.

13 All these people were still living by faith when they died. They did not receive the things promised; they only saw them and welcomed them from a distance, admitting that they were foreigners and strangers on earth. 14 People who say such things show that they are looking for a country of their own. 15 If they had been thinking of the country they had left, they would have had opportunity to return. 16 Instead, they were longing for a better country — a heavenly one. Therefore, God is not ashamed to be called their God, for he has prepared a city for them.

17 By faith Abraham, when God tested him, offered Isaac as a sacrifice. He who had embraced the promises was about to sacrifice his one and only son, 18 even though God had said to him, "It is through Isaac that your offspring will be reckoned." 19 Abraham reasoned that God could even raise the dead, and so in a manner of speaking he did receive Isaac back from death.

20 By faith Isaac blessed Jacob and Esau in regard to their future.

21 By faith Jacob, when he was dying, blessed each of Joseph's sons, and worshiped as he leaned on the top of his staff.

22 By faith Joseph, when his end was near, spoke about the exodus of the Israelites from Egypt and gave instructions concerning the burial of his bones.

23 By faith Moses' parents hid him for three months after he was born, because they saw he was no ordinary child, and they were not afraid of the king's edict.

24 By faith Moses, when he had grown up, refused to be known as the son of Pharaoh's daughter. 25 He chose to be mistreated along with the people of God rather than to enjoy the fleeting pleasures of sin. 26 He regarded disgrace for the sake of Christ as of greater value than the treasures of Egypt, because he was looking ahead to his reward. 27 By faith he left Egypt, not fearing the king's anger; he persevered because he saw him who is invisible. 28 By faith he kept the Passover and the application of blood, so that the destroyer of the firstborn would not touch the firstborn of Israel.

29 By faith the people passed through the Red Sea as on dry land; but when the Egyptians tried to do so, they were drowned.

30 By faith the walls of Jericho fell, after the army had marched around them for seven days.

31 By faith the prostitute Rahab, because she welcomed the spies, was not killed with those who were disobedient.

32 And what more shall I say? I do not have time to tell about Gideon, Barak, Samson and Jephthah, about David and Samuel and the prophets, 33 who through faith conquered kingdoms, administered justice, and gained what was promised; who shut the mouths of lions,

34 quenched the fury of the flames, and escaped the edge of the sword; whose weakness was turned to strength; and who became powerful in battle and routed foreign armies.

35 Women received back their dead, raised to life again. There were others who were tortured, refusing to be released so that they might gain an even better resurrection.
36 Some faced jeers and flogging, and even chains and imprisonment. 37 They were put to death by stoning; they were sawed in two; they were killed by the sword. They went about in sheepskins and goatskins, destitute, persecuted and mistreated — 38 the world was not worthy of them. They wandered in deserts and mountains, living in caves and in holes in the ground.

39 These were all commended for their faith, yet none of them received what had been promised, 40 since God had planned something better for us so that only together with us would they be made perfect.

INTRODUCTION

It was following the American War Between the States that a day was instituted as the American Memorial Day. It is a time for remembering those who have fallen. There is something good and noble about remembering. Hebrews 11 is a Christian memorial. It stands as a memorial to those who took a stand in faith. Let's go on a journey together for the next 40 days and discover what God says about how to live by faith!

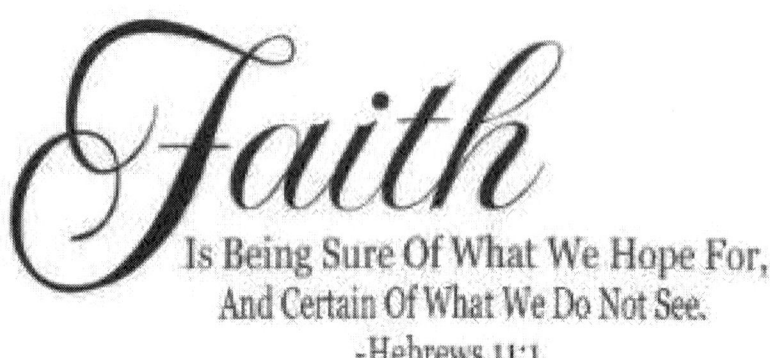

OUTLINE OF HEBREWS

J. Sidlow Baxter once said that "Hebrews is one of the greatest two theological treatises in the New Testament". Here is Baxter's outline of Hebrews:

1. JESUS - THE NEW AND "BETTER "DELIVERER (Heb 1-7).

Jesus the God-Man - better than angels (Heb 1:1-2:18).
Jesus the new Apostle - better than Moses (Heb 3:1-19)
Jesus the new Leader - better than Joshua (Heb 4:1-13).
Jesus the new priest - better than Aaron (Heb 4:14-7).

2. CALVARY - THE NEW AND "BETTER" COVENANT (Heb 8:1-10:18)

New covenant has better promises (Heb 8:6-13).
And it opens up a better sanctuary (Heb 9:1-14).
And is sealed by a better sacrifice (Heb 9:15-28).
And it achieves far better results (Heb 10:1-18).

3. FAITH - THE TRUE AND "BETTER" PRINCIPLE (Heb 10:19-13).

Faith the true response to these "better" things (Heb 10:19-39
It has always been vindicated as such: examples - Heb 11
Is now to endure, patiently looking to Jesus (Heb 12:1-13).
Is to express itself in practical sanctity (Heb 12:14-13:21).
Parting words Heb 13:22-25.

From Explore the Book - It is a recommended resource

HEBREWS CHAPTER 11
Verse by Verse

DAY 1 – Heb. 11:1

"Now faith is confidence in what we hope for and assurance about what we do not see."

Translations of Heb. 11:1:

Amplified: NOW FAITH is the assurance (the confirmation, the title deed) of the things [we] hope for, being the proof of things [we] do not see and the conviction of their reality [faith perceiving as real fact what is not revealed to the senses]. (Amplified Bible - Lockman)

Jerusalem Bible: Only faith can guarantee the blessings that we hope for, or prove the existence of the realities that at present remain unseen.

KJV: Now faith is the substance of things hoped for, the evidence of things not seen.

NLT: What is faith? It is the confident assurance that what we hope for is going to happen. It is the evidence of things we cannot yet see. (NLT - Tyndale House)

Phillips: Now faith means putting our full confidence in the things we hope for, it means being certain of things we cannot see. (Phillips: Touchstone)

Wuest: Now faith is the title deed of things hoped for, the proof of things which are not being seen. (Eerdmans)

Which translation speaks most to your heart?

_____KJV_____

Give your own definition of faith in God.

___Faith is the fundamental_____

_____

_____

Cite 3 examples of how you have trusted God in your life:

1.

2.

3.

*Warren Wiersbe adds that Hebrews 11:1 is "not a **definition of faith but a description of what faith does and how it works**. True Bible faith is not blind optimism or a manufactured "hope-so" feeling. Neither is it an intellectual assent to a doctrine. It is certainly not believing in spite of evidence! That would be superstition.*

True Bible faith is confident obedience to God's Word in spite of circumstances and consequences.

For centuries the islands of New Zealand were unpopulated. *No human had ever set foot on them. Then the first settlers arrived. They were Polynesians from other Pacific islands who had sailed a thousand miles in outrigger canoes (Maori). The Polynesians came with the purpose of settling in New Zealand. How did they know the land was there? How did they know they would not simply sail across empty seas until food and water ran out and they perished? - The Polynesians had known for generations that land was there because their voyagers had seen a long white cloud on the distant horizon. They knew that when a cloud stayed in one place over a very long period of time, there was land beneath it. They called New Zealand the Land of the Long White Cloud. Faith is like that. It is voyaging to an unseen land, journeying to an unknown future.*

Faith is believing that God will keep His promises, *despite circumstances that seem to be to the contrary! True faith that saves one's soul includes at least three main elements*

(1) firm persuasion or firm conviction

(2) a surrender to that truth

(3) a conduct emanating from that surrender

Faith is the means by which we are able to "see" this invisible world. *That is belief's true function. Faith is to the spiritual realm what the five senses are to the natural realm. The writer of Hebrews says that faith is "the evidence of things not seen" (Hebrews 11:1). By faith we recognize the existence of the spiritual world and learn to depend on the Lord for His help in our daily life. Our goal, then, as George MacDonald once said, is to "grow eyes" to see the unseen.*

At times our fears may loom so large,
We long for proof that God is near;
It's then our Father says to us,
"Have faith, My child, and do not fear."

WHAT IS THE NUMBER ONE THING YOU ARE TRUSTING GOD FOR IN YOUR LIFE RIGHT NOW?

Faith

Daring the Soul to go Beyond what the eye can See

DAY 2 – Heb. 11:2

NLT: God gave his approval to people in days of old because of their faith. (NLT - Tyndale House)

Wuest - "Men of old" used here instead of the more common expression, "the fathers," refers to the saints of the Old Testament dispensation, many of whose names are recorded in this chapter.

List some of the "elders" in your life who preceded you in life and showed you how to trust God by faith. Maybe it is a parent, grandparent, pastor or friend. Who is it that went before you and showed the path of trusting God?

_____

_____

_____

_____

_____

I have always taught as a Pastor that everyone in the Family of God ought to have 3 key people in their life:

1. **A PAUL** – *who goes before you*

2. **A BARNABAS** – *who walks beside you*

3. **A TIMOTHY** – *who follows after you*

Who is your Paul? _____

Who is your Barnabas? _____

Who is your Timothy? _____

Thank God for each person you listed.
If that person is alive, pray for God to bless them today.

REMEMBER:
Reputation is what other men think about you. Character is what God knows to be true about you. H W Beecher said that "Reputation is sometimes as wide as the horizon when character is the point of a needle."

IN THE BEGINNING, GOD CREATED THE HEAVENS AND THE EARTH.

Genesis 1:1 ESV

DAY 3 – Heb. 11:3

Translations of verse 3:

NLT: *By faith we understand that the entire universe was formed at God's command, that what we now see did not come from anything that can be seen. (NLT - Tyndale House)*

Phillips: *And it is after all only by faith that our minds accept as fact that the whole scheme of time and space was created by God's command - that the world which we can see has come into being through principles which are invisible. (Phillips: Touchstone)*

Wuest: *By means of faith we perceive that the material universe and the God-appointed ages of time were equipped and fitted by God's word for the purpose for which they were intended, and it follows therefore that that which we see did not come into being out of that which is visible. (Eerdmans)*

Young's Literal: *by faith we understand the ages to have been prepared by a saying of God, in regard to the things seen not having come out of things appearing;*

I love that phrase, "BY FAITH WE UNDERSTAND". What has faith in God in your life helped you to understand when you couldn't see it in the physical realm?

FAITH AND CREATION

Spurgeon - The facts about creation must be the subject of faith. It is true that they can be substantiated by the argument from design and in other ways; still, for a wise purpose, as I believe, God has not made even that matter of the creation of the universe perfectly clear to human reason, so there is room for the exercise of faith. Men like to have everything laid down according to the rules of mathematical precision, but God desires them to exercise faith. Therefore, He has not acted according to their wishes. Reason is all very well, but faith mounts upon the shoulders of reason and sees much farther than reason with her best telescope will ever be able to see. It is enough for us who have faith that God has told us how He made the world, and we believe it.

There are two explanations for the origin of the universe and one is total speculation, and the other is full revelation. By faith we accept the latter, the revelation that God created everything out of nothing! We weren't there when He accomplished this great feat, but He states it clearly and that is sufficient for the man or woman of faith, for God is trustworthy and His Word is true.

The fact that the author puts verse 3 at the start of his list of "by faith" examples, shows that faith in God as Creator is foundational to knowing God. The first verse of the Bible hits us squarely with a vital fact: "In the beginning God created the heavens and the earth." You cannot begin to understand yourself, other people, world history, or God if you reject the early chapters of Genesis. The first verse of Genesis presents you with a crucial choice: If God created everything that is, then He is the sovereign of the universe. If you do not come to Him in faith as your Savior, you will stand before Him in terror as your Judge! But when you believe in His Word about salvation, you gain understanding about the origins of the ages that makes everything in history fall into place.

What is your view of Genesis and the creation account?

_____

_____

What is the basis of your belief? Explain.

DAY 4 – Heb. 11:4

NLT: It was by faith that Abel brought a more acceptable offering to God than Cain did. God accepted Abel's offering to show that he was a righteous man. And although Abel is long dead, he still speaks to us because of his faith. (NLT - Tyndale House)

Note that Adam and Eve are passed over in this portion regarding creation because they had seen God, fellowshipped with Him, and talked with Him. Their children were the first to exercise faith in the unseen God but also the first to commit murder.

Kenneth Wuest nails it on this verse:

That which made Abel's sacrifice more excellent than Cain's, was not its quantity but its quality. Its quality inhered in the fact that it was the offering which God had prescribed, a blood offering. Abel had learned this from his father Adam.

The word "which" could refer grammatically either to the sacrifice or the faith. The context decides. God testified of his gifts, namely, the sacrifice. All of which means that it was by means of the blood sacrifice that he obtained witness that he was righteous.

Though Abel is dead, yet "by it" (the sacrifice) he yet speaks, telling to all that live after, that salvation is through sacrificial blood. In Heb 12:24, the statement is made that Jesus' blood speaks better things than the blood of Abel. **It is not Abel's own blood which is in view here, but the blood of the offering Abel presented to God.** *This is shown by the historical background and analysis of the epistle, the argument of which is that "The New Testament in Jesus' blood is superior to and takes the place of the First Testament in animal blood."*

The blood of Abel's offering spoke symbolically of a sacrifice for sin that God would one day offer. But Jesus' blood is the actual sacrifice, and speaks of the salvation which He procured for us on the Cross.

It was the blood offering which Abel presented to God through which he was declared righteous. This is in accord with Pauline doctrine where the great apostle speaks of "being now justified by his blood" (Ro 5:9).

Cain followed his reason and ignored revelation. He argued that his own good works as manifested by the produce which he had grown, would please God rather than a blood sacrifice. Abel accepted revelation instead, and had faith in the divine acceptability of the offering prescribed by God.

His own reason may have argued otherwise, but his faith in what God had said, won the day. Here was the example which this first-century Jew should follow in his appropriation of the salvation which Messiah procured for him on the Cross, not the way of Cain, which he had been taught by the first-century religious leaders in Israel.

LESSONS LEARNED

1. *Faith is always an obedient response to God's revelation.*

2. *Faith in God's ordained sacrifice is the only way for sinners to approach Him.*

3. *Faith in God's ordained sacrifice obtains His testimony that the sinner is righteous.*

4. *Faith in God's ordained sacrifice incurs the opposition of the self-righteous.*

5. *Faith in God's ordained sacrifice results in a life that counts for eternity.*

CONCLUSION

God accepted Abel's offering because He presented a blood sacrifice that was a portrait of the coming Savior, Jesus Christ. Cain's offering was rejected because it was a picture of his best works being presented to God for being approved of God. The Lord tells us the same today:

Titus 3:5 – *"Not by works of righteousness which we have done, but by His mercy He has saved us."*

Ephesians 2:8-9 – *"For by grace you have been saved through faith and that not of yourselves; it is the gift of God."*

GREAT QUESTION

But, Larry......how do Cain and Abel know that God wanted a lamb as an offering? It is not specified in the text in Genesis that God revealed that to them.

Yes, God did.
Adam told his sons what happened in the Garden of Eden. God found Adam and Eve in their sin and shame. Then He covered them with "coats of skin" (Gen. 3:21).

Think about it.

*Something died in the Garden of Eden.
Blood was shed to cover the sin of Adam & Eve.*

That innocent animal was a picture of the substitutionary death of Jesus Christ, the Lamb of God, who died on the Cross for our sins.

God painted a clear picture for us from the very beginning of time!!

PERSONAL QUESTION:

Which are you trusting to get into Heaven at your death:

__ I am trusting in the fact that I am basically a good person who has tried their best to please God in all that I do.

___ I am trusting in the blood that Jesus shed on the Cross for my sins as a perfect sacrifice before a perfect Heavenly Father. His blood is the substitute for my sin. That is my only hope.

Cain and Abel

DAY 5 – Heb. 11:5

Wuest: By faith Enoch was conveyed to another place, with the result that he did not see death, and he was not found because God had conveyed him to another place. For before his removal he had witness borne, that testimony still being on record, to the effect that he pleased God. (Eerdmans)

"BY FAITH" consists in receiving and believing what God has revealed. Faith according to Scofield "may be defined as that trust in the God of the Scriptures and in Jesus Christ whom He has sent, which receives Him as Lord and Savior and impels to loving obedience and good works" (John 1:12; James 2:14-26).

Here is a great quote I found from A W Tozer:
"Enoch recognized the failure of men and women trying to live their lives apart from God and His will. By faith he walked with God on this earth at a time when sin and corruption were wildly rampant all around him. Enoch's daily walk was a walk of faith, a walk of fellowship with God. What the Scriptures are trying to say to us is this:

If Enoch could live and walk with God by faith in the midst of his sinful generation, we likewise should be able to follow his example because the human race is the same and God is the same! There is only one conclusion to be drawn here. Enoch was translated into the presence of God because of his faith, and thus he escaped death. It is very evident that there was no funeral for Enoch. Those who knew him best surely had to answer many questions.

"Where is Enoch?" "What happened to Enoch?" "Why don't we see Enoch around anymore?" Perhaps members of his own family did not fully understand his walk with God, but they could answer with the facts: "He is gone! God has called him home. God has taken him." (The Tozer Topical Reader)

QUOTE FROM ARTHUR PINK

Arthur Pink sees these three figures combining to provide "an outline of the life of faith": "Abel is mentioned first not because he was born before Enoch and Noah, but because what is recorded of him in Genesis 4 illustrated and demonstrated where the life of faith begins. In like manner, Enoch is referred to next... because what was found in him... must precede that which was typified by the builder of the ark." Pink's outline traces faith's worship in Abel, faith's walk in Enoch, and faith's witness in Noah.

Two important things mark the character of Enoch's faith: (1) he pleased God by turning away from the godlessness of the world in which he lived and (2) he maintained a daily walk with God which grew so intimate that he was taken to heaven without experiencing death.

*The Genesis account (Ge 5:21, 22, 23, 24) suggests that for the first 65 years of his life, Enoch **did not walk with God**. Presumably he went along with the deteriorating morality of his times, which Genesis 6:5 describes. As Ge 5:25 suggests, the event which changed Enoch's outlook was the birth of a son, whom he named Methuselah. Some scholars derive the meaning of Methuselah from the Hebrew root muth, which means "death," and translate the name "His death shall bring (it)."*

The Genesis account states that from the birth of Methuselah throughout the following 300 years, Enoch "walked with God." This turn in his life was a result of faith, and since faith always requires a word from God to rest upon (Ro 10:17), it emphasizes the truth that Enoch was given a revelation of Christ (we cannot speculate further), and possibly a revelation of coming judgment which changed his life.

*Did you know that the name of his son, Methuselah, could be translated as: **"WHEN HE DIES, IT WILL COME"**. What a clear warning from God! Methusaleh is the only person to connect all of the way from Adam to Noah because he lived over 900 years. He is a picture of the long-lasting mercy of God for sinners.*

SOMETHING TO CONSIDER:

- *Enoch is a picture of the believer who will be raptured when Jesus calls for His Church to come Home (I Thess. 4:13-18).*

- *Enoch was raptured before the judgment fell on the earth, just as the Church will be removed and then the Tribulation will come (Rev. 3:10, II Thessalonians 2).*

ARE YOU WALKING WITH GOD?

To walk with God means that our lives are in step with God, yielded in obedience to Him, headed in the direction He chooses. Walking also implies intimacy and fellowship. Walking with a friend is a time to talk, to get to know one another, and to share the things that are happening in your lives. Walking with God is a daily process of growing more intimate with Him as you share everything in your life with Him and learn more of His ways.

Of course, you have to do your own walking. Someone else can't do it for you. Just as a physical exercise program requires discipline, so spiritual walking requires discipline (1Ti 4:7-note). You have to take the initiative, the time, and the effort that is required to walk with God. If you don't make frequent appointments to get alone with Him, it won't happen.

If you don't make an effort to read His Word and apply it to your life, you're not walking with Him. If you are not memorizing His promises and applying them to the various situations you face, you're not walking by faith. If you have trusted in Christ as Savior, but you have grown lazy and aren't walking with Him, then get up and get back on the path. Faith is a daily dependence on God, step by step, that continues over a lifetime.

PERSONAL QUESTIONS:

What area of your life most pleases God at this time?

_____

_____

What area of your life least pleases God at this time?

> I have a great need for Christ. I have a great Christ for my need.
>
> — Charles Spurgeon

DAY 6 – Heb. 11:6

Phillips: And without faith it is impossible to please him. The man who approaches God must have faith in two things, first that God exists and secondly that it is worth a man's while to try to find God. (Phillips: Touchstone).

"WITHOUT FAITH" *- Barnes comments that this signifies confidence in God's fidelity, His truth, His wisdom, and His promises.*

And this is as true in other things as in our faith. It is impossible for a child to please his father unless he has confidence in him. It is impossible for a wife to please her husband, or a husband a wife, unless they have confidence in each other. If there is distrust and jealousy on either part, there is discord and misery.

We cannot be pleased with a professed friend unless he has such confidence in us as to believe our declarations and promises. **The same thing is true of God.** *He cannot be pleased with the man who has no confidence in Him; who doubts the truth of His declarations and promises; who does not believe that His ways are right, or that He is qualified for universal empire.*

"The requirement of faith or confidence in God is not arbitrary; it is just what we require of our children, and partners in life, and friends, as the indispensable condition of our being pleased with them." (Albert Barnes. Barnes NT Commentary)

Charles Swindoll commenting on faith and obedience in John 3:36 concludes that…

"In 3:36 the one who "believes in the Son has eternal life" as a present possession. But the one who "does not obey the Son shall not see life." To disbelieve Christ is to disobey Him. And logically, to believe in Christ is to obey Him. This verse clearly indicates that belief is not a matter of passive opinion, but decisive and obedient action."

Tragically, many people are convinced that it doesn't really matter what you believe, so long as you are sincere. This reminds me of a Peanuts cartoon in which Charlie Brown is returning from a disastrous baseball game. The caption read, "174 to nothing! How could we lose when we were so sincere?"

The reality is, Charlie Brown, that it takes more than sincerity to win the game of life. Many people are sincere about their beliefs, but they are sincerely wrong!" (Swindoll, C. R., & Zuck, R. B. Understanding Christian Theology.: Thomas Nelson Publishers)

Here is an awesome comment on faith by Adrian Rogers!

"You see, by faith, man gives God pleasure. Our faith pleases God and through faith God gives man treasure. According to your faith, be it unto you. Faith is the medium of exchange in the kingdom of heaven, just like money is the medium of exchange. If you want to go to the grocery store, you buy something, it takes money. You come to heaven to receive from God, "Without faith it's impossible to please him, for he that comes to God must believe that he is and that he is a rewarder of them that diligently seek him. According to your faith be it unto you."

In order to please God four things must concur, all of which are accomplished by faith.

First, the person of him *that pleases God must be accepted of Him (Ge. 4:4).*

Secondly, the thing done *that pleases God must be in accord with His will (He 13:21).*

Thirdly, the manner of doing *it must be pleasing to God: it must be performed in humility (1Co 15:10), in sincerity (Is 38:3), in cheerfulness (2Co 8:12; 9:7).*

Fourthly, the end in view must be God's glory (1Co 10:31). Now faith is the only means whereby these four requirements are met.

GREAT ILLUSTRATION

In his book, Your God is Too Small, J. B. Phillips describes some of the common gods that people manufacture. One is the grand old man god, the grandfatherly, white-haired, indulgent god who smiles down on men and winks at their adultery, stealing, cheating, and lying. Then there are the resident policeman god, whose primary job is to make life difficult and unenjoyable, and the god in a box, the private and exclusive sectarian god. The managing director god is the god of the deists, the god who designed and created the universe, started it spinning, and now stands by far away watching it run down. God is not pleased with belief in any of these idolatrous substitutes."

QUESTION: Should the believer in Christ be motivated by rewards in heaven? Why not? Is God Himself the totality of our reward?

_____

_____

LET YOUR **FAITH** BE BIGGER THAN YOUR **FEARS**

DAY 7 – Heb. 11:7

NLT: It was by faith that Noah built an ark to save his family from the flood. He obeyed God, who warned him about something that had never happened before. By his faith he condemned the rest of the world and was made right in God's sight. (NLT - Tyndale House)

Noah obeyed at all costs. To build the huge vessel must have cost Noah a great deal of money and labor. He could not get everybody to work at the absurd task of building a vessel on dry land. As they would be laughed at, his workmen would be sure to demand extra pay. Possibly he had to pay double wages to everyone employed on the ark.

This patriarch of the faith was content to sink all his capital and all his income in this singular venture. It was a poor speculation – so everybody told him – and yet he was quite willing to put all his eggs into that one basket. God had told him to build, and build he would, feeling that the divine command insured him against risk.

Can we do the same? When you have trusted God against all odds?

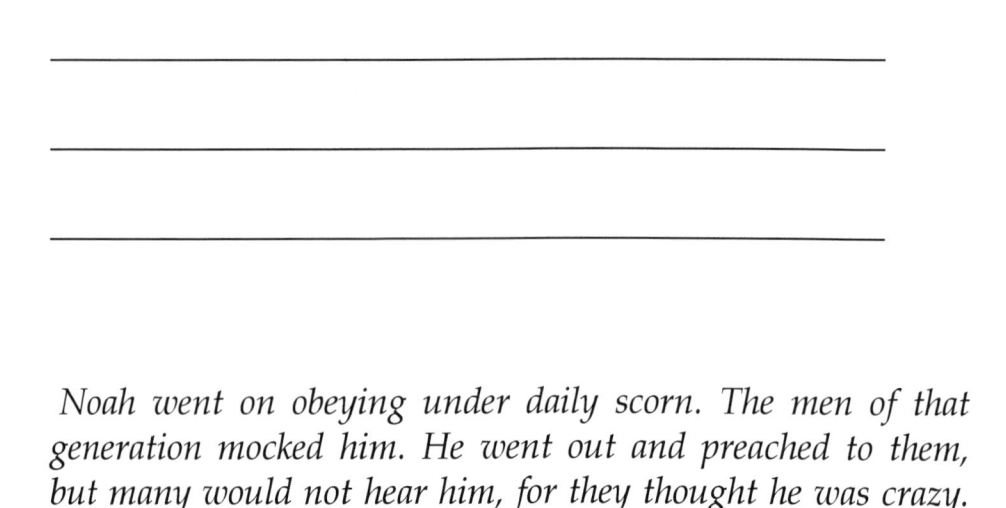

Noah went on obeying under daily scorn. The men of that generation mocked him. He went out and preached to them, but many would not hear him, for they thought he was crazy. Those who did listen to him said to each other, "He is building a vessel upon dry land – is he insane? There had never been a flood. There was no scientific basis for his belief!

Those critics of this genius of faith are all dead and forgotten now. We don't even know their names! But Noah is remembered still in GOD'S HALL OF FAITH in Hebrews chapter 11!

THE DAYS OF NOAH
Christ has warned us that He is coming again and his return will come at a time when it is like the days of Noah (Matthew 24).

How is our world like Noah's? _____

_____

_____

_____

Who have you warned of the return of Christ?

_____

_____

_____

What does it cost you to serve the Lord like it did Noah?

_____

_____

Do you have family members or friends who feel that you condemn them when they look at the way you live your life?

_____

_____

_____

Pray for them now by name before the Lord. Ask the Holy Spirit to convict them of their need of a Savior and pray for them to turn to Christ.

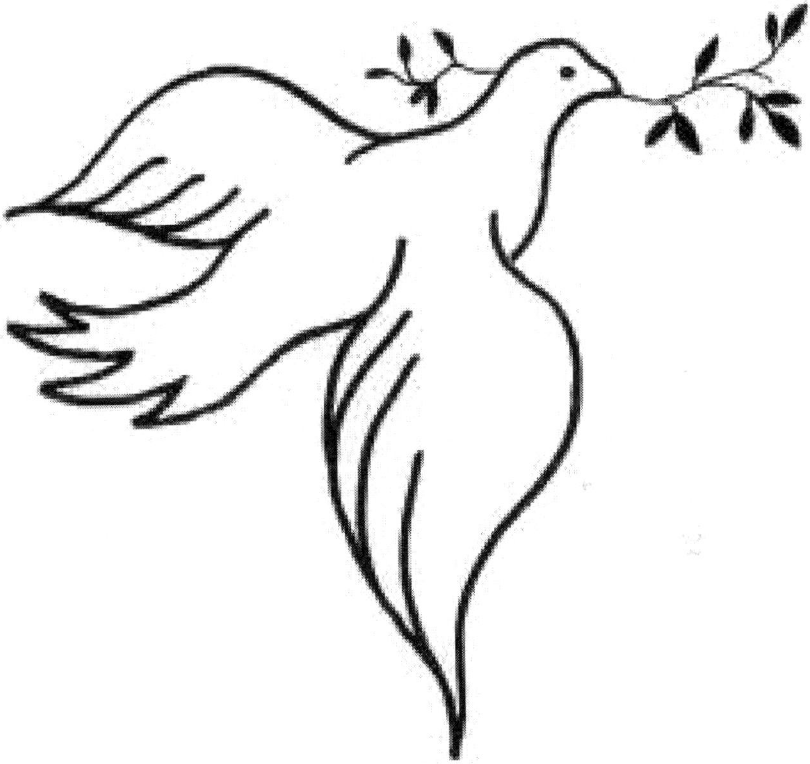

DAY 8 – Heb. 11:8

Wuest: By faith Abraham, while he was being called, obeyed to go out into a place which he was about to be receiving as an inheritance, and he went out, not troubling his mind as to where he was going. (Eerdmans)

ABRAHAM LISTENED TO GOD'S VOICE.
The Book of Hebrews is all about hearing God's voice. Check out these passages of Scripture:

Hebrews 2:1: For this reason we must pay much closer attention to what we have heard, lest we drift away from it.

Hebrews 3:7: Therefore, just as the Holy Spirit says, "TODAY IF YOU HEAR HIS VOICE, Do not harden your hearts....as in day of trial in the wilderness."

Hebrews 3:15: "While it is said, "TODAY IF YOU HEAR HIS VOICE, Do not harden your hearts, as when they provoked Me."

Hebrews 4:7 – "He again fixes a certain day, "Today," saying through David after so long a time just as has been said before, "TODAY IF YOU HEAR HIS VOICE, DO NOT HARDEN YOUR HEARTS."

If God repeats Himself three times......you really ought to listen, don't you think!

Hebrews 5:9 – *"And having been made perfect, He became to all those who obey (literally "hear under", listen attentively hupakouo = hupo + akouo) Him the source of eternal salvation."*

Hebrews 5:11 – *"Concerning him we have much to say, and it is hard to explain, since you have become dull of HEARING."*

Hebrews 11:8 – *"By faith Abraham, when he was called, obeyed (literally "hear under", listen attentively hupakouo = hupo + akouo) by going out to a place which he was to receive for an inheritance; and he went out, not knowing where he was going."*

PERSONAL APPLICATION

Abraham heard God's voice and followed Him. What have you heard God call you to do that you have not yet obeyed?

_____

_____

_____

_____

Vance Havner, one of my favorites, has an incredible comment on the faith of Abraham that I just absolutely love!

"Abraham went out, not knowing where he was going. When God calls us to the adventure of faith, He does not furnish a road-map in advance. We have a sinking feeling of having stepped out on nothing, **but then God is always doing wonderful things with nothing: He hangs the earth on nothing (Job 26:7), and calls those things which are not as though they were.**

Neither does faith know why. Habakkuk wondered: "O Lord... why?" (Hab 1:2, 3). So did Job. God did not give them explanation but revelation, and when they saw God they did not need explanation. When we see whom, the why does not matter.

Faith does not know what. Peter was concerned about John: "What shall this man do?" Our Lord never explains the whats: "What I do thou knowest not now; but thou shalt know hereafter" (John 13:7).

 But one thing faith does know: "I know whom I have believed." (2 Tim. 1:12) He knows the wheres, whys, and whats: "He knoweth the way that I take" (Job 23:10-note). Sight rests on some thing, some where; faith rests upon someone, anywhere! (2Cor 5:7)

*The world crowns quick success;
God crowns long-term faithfulness.*

><>><>><>

DAY 9 -- Heb. 11:9

Phillips: It was faith that kept him journeying like a foreigner through the land of promise, with no more home than the tents which he shared with Isaac and Jacob, co-heirs with him of the promise. (Phillips: Touchstone)

Abraham was a man who put his faith in ACTION! Faith without works is dead (James 2:14-18). How have you acted on your faith recently?

_____

_____

_____

_____

_____

What is the best example of faith in action that you have seen or heard about recently?

_____

_____

_____

_____

"AS IN A FOREIGN LAND" - *In other words Abraham lived like a foreigner, which is how all believers should live their short time on earth -- as "aliens and foreigners" (1Pe 2:11).*

Are you "tethered" to this world which is passing away (1Jn 2:17)? If so, consider Abraham's example. Remember he was able to live in the temporal the way he lived because he was looking for the eternal while in the temporal. Set your mind on the things above dear short timer" saint! (Col 3:14).

Abraham is in three things a pattern to us who believe; and those three things will be the divisions of our subject to-night. He is a pattern to us, first, in the mode of his living: "He sojourned in the land of promise, as in a strange country, dwelling in tents."

Secondly, Abraham is a pattern to believers in the company he kept: "With Isaac and Jacob, the heirs with him of the same promise."

And, thirdly, Abraham is a pattern to believers in the home he looked for: "For he looked for a city which hath foundations, whose builder and maker is God." (Hebrews 11:9, 10 Abraham, A Pattern to Believers).

This world is not my Home
I'm just passing through.
My treasures are laid up
Somewhere beyond the blue!

DAY 10 - Heb. 11:10

KJV: For he looked for a city which hath foundations, whose builder and maker is God.

I have often been intrigued by the phrase, "a city which has no foundations." That's the kind of home Abraham was searching for all those years. It seems like such a strange verse at times. What does it mean?

CHARLES SPURGEON – This great quote by the prince of preachers from London speaks volumes to my heart. I hope it touches yours as well!

"Abraham used to pull up the tent pins, and his men would take down the big tent pole, and roll up the canvas, and they were soon away, always moving about that country with their flocks and herds. The tents had no foundations, but Abraham was looking for a city that had foundations. **There is nothing on earth that really has a foundation that is lasting**. Even those buildings that seem most firm will be dissolved, and burned up in the last general fire. All things here pass away.

When we are most comfortable as believers here in a foreign land, we may hear a voice saying, "Up and away: pack up your tent, and journey somewhere else." Sit loose by this world, I pray you.

And all of God's people say? AMEN. That's an amazing quote.

WHAT DID ABRAHAM HAVE?

If following God's call is a challenge for us, imagine how it was for Abraham, who had no Bible, no pastor, no sermons, no commentaries, and no Christian encouragement or accountability. But what he did have was the promise of a nation, a land, and a blessing (Gen. 12:1–3). That was good enough for him. All he had to bank his faith upon was THE WORD OF GOD!

And that is the same thing we have today.
We are no different than Abraham.
God is no different today.
The promises of God are just as sure today.
Heaven is just as real today!

Though we are to be looking forward to our heavenly home, that does not mean that we are to be so "heavenly minded" that we are of no earthly value!

In his book Mere Christianity, C. S. Lewis wrote, "If you read history you will find that the Christians who did the most for the present world were just those who thought most of the next. The apostles themselves, . . . the great men who built up the Middle Ages, the English evangelicals who abolished the slave trade, all left their mark on earth, precisely because their minds were occupied with heaven. It is since Christians have largely ceased to think of the other world that they have become so ineffective in this. Aim at heaven and you will get earth 'thrown in.'"

THINKING ABOUT HEAVEN

Who are you looking forward to seeing in Heaven one day?

_____

_____

_____

_____

Who in your life does not have a home in Heaven and needs you to stay here for a while longer and point them Home?

_____

_____

_____

_____

What are you doing to reach that friend or family member for Christ? One day it will be too late.

DAY 11 - Heb. 11:11

Barclay: *It was by faith that Sarah, too, received power to conceive and to bear a son, although she was beyond the age for it, for she believed that he who gave the promise could be absolutely relied upon. (Westminster Press)*

Amplified: *Because of faith also Sarah herself received physical power to conceive a child, even when she was long past the age for it, because she considered [God] Who had given her the promise to be reliable and trustworthy and true to His word. (Amplified Bible - Lockman)*

This woman of faith, Sarah, is enrolled among these saintly ones. Her faith was not all it should have been. She laughed in God's face! But God saw HER heart and looked at her whole life, not just one mistake. He wrote the record and put her in His HALL OF FAITH, anyway. God is so merciful!

One translator says of Hebrews 11:11 that this verse could actually say that Sarah was at the **"PROPER TIME"** *in God's view, as the writer of Hebrews uses the awesome Greek word, karios. It means a "point in time or period of time" It means "just the right moment in time."*

Kairos can refer to a fixed and definite time, the time when things are brought to crisis.

Kairos is not so much a succession of minutes, but a period of OPPORTUNITY. In other words, kairos defines the best time to do something, the moment when circumstances are most suitable, the "ripe" moment.

What OPPORTUNITY or kairos moment has God opened for you to walk through recently?

_____

_____

_____

_____

_____

What opportunity are you praying for God to open that He has not granted you yet?

_____

NOW FAITH IS BEING SURE OF WHAT WE HOPE FOR AND CERTAIN OF WHAT WE DO NOT SEE.
HEBREWS 11:1
HOPEFOR

DAY 12 – Heb. 11:12

Amplified: So from one man, though he was physically as good as dead, there have sprung descendants whose number is as the stars of heaven and as countless as the innumerable sands on the seashore. (*Amplified Bible - Lockman*)

Here is one of the greatest illustrations of how faith in action brings the favor of God.

George Muller of Bristol exemplified the nitty-gritty of a life of faith. After being a wild youth, he was converted in his early twenties. He obeyed God's call by living a life of faith and obedience. He lived in a manner that the world could not fathom. He and his wife sold all of their earthly possessions, founded an orphanage, and lived by faith alone, making their needs and those of the orphans known only to God in prayer. They often faced insurmountable problems that were overcome by faith in God's power.

In 1877, Muller was on board a ship that was stalled off the coast of Newfoundland in dense fog. The captain had been on the bridge for 24 hours when Muller came to see him. Muller told him that he had to be in Quebec by Saturday afternoon. The captain replied, "It is impossible."

"Very well," said Muller, "if your ship cannot take me, God will find some other way-I have never broken an engagement for 52 years. Let's go down to the chart room and pray." The captain wondered what lunatic asylum Muller had escaped from.

"Mr. Muller," he said, "do you know how dense this fog is?"

"No, my eye is not on the density of the fog, but on the living God, Who controls every circumstance of my life."

Muller knelt down and prayed simply. When he had finished, the captain was about to pray, but Muller put his hand on his shoulder, and told him not to: "First, you do not believe He will; and second, I believe He has, and there is no need whatever for you to pray about it." The captain looked at Muller in amazement.

"Captain," he continued, "I have known my Lord for 52 years, and there has never been a single day that I have failed to get an audience with the King. Get up, captain, and open the door, and you will find the fog is gone." The captain walked across to the door and opened it. The fog had lifted. (From, Roger Steer, George Muller: Delighted in God [Harold Shaw Publishers], p. 243.)

QUESTION FOR TODAY:

Where are you trusting God to provide for you something which is beyond your ability to answer???

_____

_____

DAY 13 – Heb. 11:13

NLT: *All these faithful ones died without receiving what God had promised them, but they saw it all from a distance and welcomed the promises of God. They agreed that they were no more than foreigners and nomads here on earth.* (NLT - Tyndale House)

"IN FAITH" - Literally this reads "according to faith." What does this mean? Vine comments that the idea is that they died "in keeping with their life of faith." And so they died, as they lived. Wuest feels that the idea is that "These all died dominated by faith." That is their strong, persevering faith was a controlling characteristic of their life.

THEY DIED WITHOUT RECEIVING ALL.

These Old Testament saints that the writer of Hebrews refers to here received a great deal of revelation from God, but they had not received the fullness of His promises.

Abraham had not beheld his seed so many as the sands upon the seashore.

Neither Isaac nor Jacob had ever seen the Shiloh, in whom all the nations of the earth are blessed. No, they had not received the promises.

And you and I have not received all the promises of God yet, either.. We have received a great deal, but there are *certain promises that we have not received. The glorious coming of our Lord Jesus Christ, which is the brightest hope of the church, when the Lord "will descend from heaven with a shout of command, with the voice of the archangel and with the trumpet of God" (1Th 4:16) – we have not received that as yet.*

Heaven itself, with all its splendor, its white robes and palms of victory, we have not yet received. *We are looking for these. We die in faith, expecting that we shall enter upon the fulfillment of these promises.*

THREE TENSES OF FAITH

Dying in faith has distinct reference to the past. *They believed the promises which had gone before, and were assured that their sins were blotted out through the mercy of God.*

Dying in faith has to do with the present. *These saints were confident of their acceptance with God, they enjoyed the beams of his love, and rested in his faithfulness.*

Dying in faith looks into the future. *They fell asleep, affirming that the Messiah would surely come, and that when He would in the last days appear upon the earth, they would rise from their graves to behold Him. To them the pains of death were but the birth-pangs of a better state.*

FOUR FACTS OF FAITH

1. *We must see God's promises* - *Before we can believe in God's promises, we must see them. Before we can see them,*

God must open our spiritually blind eyes (Mt. 13:11, 12, 13, 14, 15).

2. We must welcome God's promises - *Having seen God's promises, the patriarchs **welcomed them**. (KJV and NKJV add that they were persuaded or assured of the promises, but there is virtually no manuscript evidence for this reading.) They greeted God's promises with open arms. They brought God's promises into their lives as gladly as welcomed guests into their tents.* **Have you done that? Have you welcomed Jesus Christ into your life as Savior and Lord? Have you embraced Him as you would a long lost friend?**

3. We can only see and welcome the promises from a distance - *What does this mean? It amplifies the opening phrase of the verse, that these men "died in faith, without receiving the promises." But, Hebrews 6:15-note states, "having patiently waited, [Abraham] obtained the promise." Hebrews 11:17 says that Abraham "had received the promises."*

THE WORLD SAYS, "What a joke! That's "pie in the sky when you die"! The world says, "I want cash in the stash here and now, not pie in the sky when I die!"

But, as C. S. Lewis observed (The Problem of Pain [Macmillan], pp. 132-133):

Scripture habitually put the joys of heaven into the scale against the sufferings of earth, and no solution of the problem of pain which does not do so can be called a Christian one. We are very shy nowadays of even mentioning heaven. We are afraid of the jeer about "pie in the sky,"

But either there is "pie in the sky" or there is not. If there is not, then Christianity is false, for this doctrine is woven into its whole fabric. So, we must see and welcome God's promises, although we can only do so in this life from a distance.

4. Seeing and welcoming God's promises alienates us from this world - *The reason that Abraham left his homeland and migrated to Canaan was that he had seen and welcomed God's promises. If he had ignored God's promises, he would have continued to live in his native land, where he blended in with everyone else. But be-cause he believed God and obeyed His call, he went out from his family and friends and "lived as an alien in the land of promise, as in a foreign land, dwelling in tents with Isaac and Jacob, fellow heirs of the same promise" (He 11:9-note).*

THE ULTIMATE TEST OF FAITH IS NOT HOW LOUDLY YOU PRAISE GOD IN happy times but HOW DEEPLY YOU TRUST HIM IN DARK TIMES

DAY 15 - Heb. 11:15

Amplified: *If they had been thinking with [homesick] remembrance of that country from which they were emigrants, they would have found constant opportunity to return to it. (Amplified Bible - Lockman).*

KJV: *And truly, if they had been mindful of that country from whence they came out, they might have had opportunity to have returned.*

NLT: *If they had meant the country they came from, they would have found a way to go back. (NLT - Tyndale House)*

Phillips: *If they had meant the particular country they had left behind, they had ample opportunity to return. (Phillips: Touchstone)*

Wuest: *And if indeed they had been remembering that country from which they had gone out, in that case they would have had constant opportunity to bend their way back again.* (**Eerdmans**)

Young's Literal: *and if, indeed, they had been mindful of that from which they came forth, they might have had an opportunity to return,*

"IF THEY HAD BEEN THINKING OF THAT COUNTRY"

- This phrase emphasizes that the battle of whether we live in the world but not of the world is always in our mind. **Lord, keep me seeking and setting my mind on things above (Col 3:1-2):**

"Since, then, you have been raised with Christ, set your hearts on things above, where Christ is, seated at the right hand of God. ² Set your minds on things above, not on earthly things. ³ For you died, and your life is now hidden with Christ in God. ⁴ When Christ, who is your[a] life, appears, then you also will appear with him in glory."

PERSONAL QUESTION

Do you ever think about walking away from your faith as a Christian?

_____

_____

Isn't that what Lot's wife did? She couldn't forget the pleasures of a sinful city and looked back. Would you go back to your life before Christ right now if you could?

_____

_____

_____

_____

Jesus' call to remember Lot's wife conveys a serious, sobering warning to all who would seek to follow Him. In a sense, His charge to "Remember Lot's wife" serves as a test of the bent or direction of our heart - "Is our heart generally going in a world-ward or a God-ward direction?"

THOUGHT:

Are we genuine followers of Christ, truly disciples, (John 8:31) or are we like those who wanted the physical bread from Christ but did not desire the Bread from heaven and turned back from following the Savior?

Can you say?

I have decided to follow Jesus.
NO TURNING BACK.

Though none go with me, yet still I'll follow.
NO TURNING BACK.

Take this whole world, just give me Jesus!
NO TURNING BACK.

DAY 16 - Heb. 11:16

NLT: *But they were looking for a better place, a heavenly homeland. That is why God is not ashamed to be called their God, for he has prepared a heavenly city for them.* (<u>NLT - Tyndale House</u>).

Steven Cole says about Hebrews that *"the author is writing to people who were encountering hardships in their new life as Christians (or least those who professed to be Christians). They were tempted to go back to their old religion. So he points out that the patriarchs could have returned to Mesopotamia if they had been looking for an earthly inheritance. The living conditions in their former homeland were probably far more developed than in the land of Canaan. If they had returned, their family and friends would have welcomed them with open arms, whereas in Canaan, they were kept at a distance. But they endured the hardships and didn't go back because they were seeking* **a better country, that is, a heavenly one**. (<u>He 11:16</u>)

The application is that as believers, we must make a break from our old life and from the world.

THINK ABOUT IT.

An article in a San Francisco newspaper reported that a young man who once found a $5 bill on the street resolved that from that time on he would never lift his eyes while walking. The paper went on to say that over the years he accumulated, *among other things, 29,516 buttons, 54,172 pins, 12 cents, a bent back, and a miserly disposition. But he also lost something—the glory of sunlight, the radiance of the stars, the smiles of friends, and the freshness of blue skies. I'm afraid that some Christians are like that man. While they may not walk around staring at the sidewalk, they are so engrossed with the things of this life that they give little attention to spiritual and eternal values. Perhaps they've gotten a taste of some fleeting pleasure offered by the world and they've been spending all their time pursuing it (Eccl 1:14, 12:1, 8, 13,14). But that is dangerous.*

Personal Questions

1. *How do you define the word, "WORLDLINESS"? What does that mean in your life?*

   _____

   _____

   _____

   _____

2. *What is the balance between being distinct from the world and, yet, relating to the world enough to be a witness?*

_____

_____

_____

_____

_____

3. *How can we develop a deeper desire for Heaven?*

_____

_____

_____

_____

_____

DAY 17 - Heb. 11:17

Barclay: *It was by faith that Abraham offered up Isaac when he was put to the test. He was willing to offer up even his only son, (Westminster Press).*

Dwight Pentecost *commenting on Abraham's faith and obedience exemplified in Hebrews 11:17-19 writes that "Our faith is often tested most when our present circumstances seem completely contrary to what God has revealed to us through His Word. That is precisely the situation Abraham faced, and yet he did not succumb to "doubting in the dark what God told him in the light." Instead, he lived his life in accordance with what God had said. (Pentecost, J. D., & Durham, K.. Faith that Endures: A Practical Commentary on the Book of Hebrews. Grand Rapids, MI: Kregel Publication).*

This event in the Old Testament is the only DOUBLE-TYPE recorded in one biblical event. *Here we see portraits or types of the Father and the Son:*

* **Abraham is a portrait of God the Father who gave His only begotten Son.**

* **Isaac is a type of Christ the Son who was obedient even to the death of the Cross.**

* *The Ram caught by its thorns in the thicket is a type of Christ who was caught by the thorns of my sin and became my Subsitute at Calvary.*

The fourth stanza (below) of one of the grand old hymns, <u>Trust and Obey</u>, captures the essence of Abraham's sacrifice:

When we walk with the Lord in the light of His Word,
What a glory He sheds on our way!
While we do His good will, He abides with us still,
And with all who will trust and obey.

Refrain
Trust and obey, for there's no other way
To be happy in Jesus, but to trust and obey.

Not a shadow can rise, not a cloud in the skies,
But His smile quickly drives it away;
Not a doubt or a fear, not a sigh or a tear,
Can abide while we trust and obey.

Not a burden we bear, not a sorrow we share,
But our toil He doth richly repay;
Not a grief or a loss, not a frown or a cross,
But is blessed if we trust and obey.

But we never can prove the delights of His love
Until all on the altar we lay;
For the favor He shows, for the joy He bestows,
Are for them who will trust and obey.

James Smith has given an excellent outline in his message, THE TRIAL OF FAITH from <u>Genesis 22:1-14</u>.

I. **The Sacrifice of Faith.** *"His only loved son" (v. 2). This simply meant his all. All must be given up to God (<u>Matt. 19:21</u>; <u>Rom. 12:1</u>, <u>2</u>; <u>15:3</u>).*

II. **The Obedience of Faith.** *"He rose up early" (v. 3). By faith he obeyed (<u>Heb. 11:7</u>). Love makes swift the feet of faith.*

III. **The Expectation of Faith.** *"I and the lad will come again" (v. 5); accounting that God was able to raise him up (<u>Heb. 11:19</u>). His promise could not fail (<u>Gen. 21:12</u>).*

IV. **The Work of Faith.** *"He laid the burden (wood) on the offering" (v. 6). Solemn work to faith. "He bore our sins in His own body on the tree" (<u>1 Peter 2:24</u>).*

V. **The Assurance of Faith.** *"God will provide" (v. 8). On the path of obedience many a question will arise (v. 7) which only faith can answer (<u>Acts 27:25</u>).*

*VI. **The Persistence of Faith**. "He bound Isaac" (v. 9). The faith that fails in the hour of trial is no faith (Mark 4:40).*

*VII. **The Victory of Faith**. "Now I know," says God, and the lad is saved; yet an offering made (v. 12), and faith abundantly rewarded (Rom. 9:33; Mark 9:25; 1 John 5:4). (Handfuls of Purpose)*

PERSONAL QUESTIONS

1. Why is it important to distinguish between testing and temptation?

_____

_____

_____

_____

2. How can we know if God is telling us to do something, or whether it is coming from some other source?

_____

_____

_____

3. Does faith mean putting our brains in neutral? How can we know when to stop trying to understand and just to trust?

4. How can we overcome the fear that God may take that which is most precious from us?

Abraham & Isaac

DAY 18 - Heb. 11:18

NLT: though God had promised him, "Isaac is the son through whom your descendants will be counted." (NLT - Tyndale House)

Spurgeon – "However puzzled Abraham may have been by the command to offer up the son in whom his seed was to be called, his plain duty was to obey that command and to leave the Lord to fulfill His own promise in His own way. Perhaps he had also learned, through his mistake concerning Ishmael, that God's way of fulfilling His promise might not be his way, and that God's way was always best. **The faith that was undismayed when the promise of a son was uttered was still undaunted when the Lord demanded the life that He had so strangely given.**"

Steven Cole sees three main points in Abraham's test:

1. God will always test our faith.

"By faith Abraham, when he was tested, offered up Isaac...." As Peter wrote (1 Pet. 1:6-7) to believers facing persecution, "In this [your salvation] you greatly rejoice, even though now for a little while, if necessary, you have been distressed by various trials, so that the proof of your faith, being more precious than gold which is perishable, even though tested by fire, may be found to result in praise and glory and honor at *the revelation of Jesus Christ." Testing through fire sounds scary, but keep in mind: God will test our faith, but never beyond what we can bear.*

Paul promises (1 Cor. 10:13), "No temptation has overtaken you but such as is common to man; and God is faithful, who will not allow you to be tempted beyond what you are able, but with the temptation will provide the way of escape also, so that you will be able to endure it." Tempted comes from the same Greek verb translated tested in Heb. 11:17.

James 1:13-14 explains, "Let no one say when he is tempted [same verb], 'I am being tempted by God'; for God cannot be tempted by evil, and He Himself does not tempt anyone. But each one is tempted when he is carried away and enticed by his own lust."

2. We should respond to the testing of our faith with prompt obedience and total surrender of that which is most precious to us.

3. Faith counts on God to keep His promises, even if it requires the humanly impossible.

PERSONAL QUESTIONS

What has God promised you that He hasn't given yet?

_____
_____
_____
_____
_____
_____

Where has God tested your faith the most?

_____
_____
_____
_____
_____
_____

Is there anything in your life that God cannot have?

_____
_____
_____
_____

DAY 19 – Heb. 11:19

NLT: *Abraham assumed that if Isaac died, God was able to bring him back to life ag ain. And in a sense, Abraham did receive his son back from the dead. (NLT - Tyndale House)*

If we consider the character of our God, we can better obey even though we don't fully understand what He is doing in our life. Abraham walked by faith, not sight. His faith "told" him that God was able to work out His purpose, even though he could not see how that could be accomplished. Have you ever been in the same situation before?

_____
_____
_____
_____

FAITH LAUGHS.

Faith laughs at impossibilities. Abraham expects that God will raise his son from the dead, or do something equally wonderful, so that the promise He had given shall be fulfilled. It was not Abraham's business to keep God's promise for Him; it was God's business to do that for Himself, and He did it.

You remember how Rebekah tried to make God's promise come true for Jacob, and what a mess she made by her plotting and scheming. When we give our attention to keeping God's Word and leave Him to fulfill His own promises, all will be well. It was Abraham's part to offer up his son; it was God's part to fulfill the promise to His seed according to the covenant that He had made.

Augustine said that "Faith is to believe what we do not see, and the reward of this faith is to see what we believe."

BIG QUESTION

What BIG thing are you believing God for right now in your life?

_____

_____

_____

REMEMBER:
If God can raise the dead……He can solve your situation.

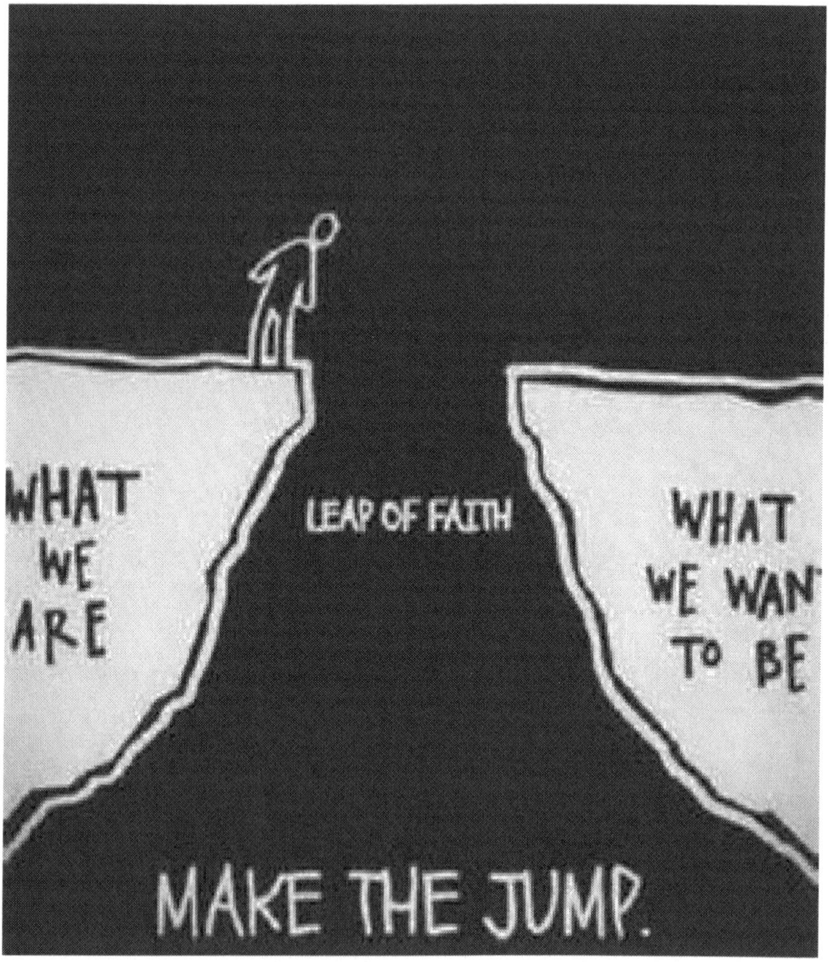
WHAT
WE
ARE
LEAP OF FAITH
WHAT
WE WANT
TO BE
MAKE THE JUMP.

Day 20 – Heb. 11:20

Phillips: It was by faith that Isaac gave Jacob and Esau his blessing, for his words dealt with what should happen in the future.   (Phillips: Touchstone)

In these next 3 verses the writer looks at the end of the lives of the next three patriarchs after Abraham to emphasize how their lives (albeit not perfect) were examples of those who remained faithful. Remember the writer is speaking primarily to Jews who are being tested and tempted to revert to Judaism and he wants these examples of perseverance to the end to encourage his readers.

Kenneth Wuest on The Blessing on Isaac:

Isaac pronounced a blessing concerning things to come," namely, things beyond the lifetime of Jacob and Esau. The blessing was an act of faith.

The Greek word for blessing is the word, eulogeo, meaning, "To say good or positive things."

Eulogeo can be from men to God, from men to men, and from God to men. When God blesses men with a blessing, He grants them favor from His throne.

WHAT IS THE BLESSING?

The Blessing is a life-changing gift of unconditional love and acceptance passed down from one generation to the next. Through the Blessing, children and adults find out what it means to be highly valued and loved by someone else by using five specific actions first laid out in the Bible:

Meaningful touch
A Spoken Message
Attaching High Value
Picturing a Special Future
An Active Commitment

By choosing to give these five incredibly simple, yet amazingly powerful "elements" of The Blessing to others, you can enrich or restore parent-child relationships, strengthen marriages, build friendships and provide a deeper understanding of God's love and blessing in our lives.

BLESSING IN MARRIAGE

Giving a blessing to our spouses will also make a profound difference in our marriages.

1. We can touch in ways that convey concern, affection, and encouragement.

2. Every day, we can speak words of admiration, gratitude, and appreciation.

3. *We can choose to attach high value to our spouses, and we can be deliberate in expressing that high value to them.*

PERSONAL QUESTIONS:

What blessings were bestowed upon you by your parents?

_____

_____

_____

_____

_____

What blessings are you missing from your parents?

_____

_____

_____

DAY 21 – Heb. 11:21

KJV: *By faith Jacob, when he was a dying, blessed both the sons of Joseph; and worshipped, leaning upon the top of his staff.*

"Jacob Worshipped" - What a way to end one's life! Worshipping. The perfect preparation for entrance into the presence of the only One Worthy of worship! Jacob's example of how to die well sets the bar high but imminently attainable by faith. Faith in the Father's promise of a forever future is the only way to truly handle the prospect of death. The patriarchs trusted in God's promised resurrection, and thus were enabled to face death with a calm serenity. How else could you describe Jacob's worshiping God while resting on his staff. Mark it down that the mark of genuine believer is their approach to death with a peace that passes all human (natural) understanding because it comes from a Supernatural Source, God Himself! Death to a believer like Jacob is exchanging a prison for a palace and a putting off of our worthless rages for His righteous robes.

Jacob's attitude was a lot like **D L Moody's** who once quipped...Some day you will read in the papers that D. L. Moody, of East Northfield, is dead. Don't you believe a word of it! At that moment I shall be more alive than I am now.

LAST WORDS OF DYING PEOPLE

President George Washington: *"Doctor, I am dying, but I am not afraid to die." He folded his hands over his chest and said: "It is well."*

Marilyn Monroe: *"I don't need your Jesus." Related by Billy Graham who tried to present the Gospel message to Marilyn, just before she died at age 36.*

Voltaire, one of history's best known atheists, *often stated that "By the time I'm buried, the Bible will be non--existent." His last words were: "I am abandoned by God and man; I shall die and go to hell alone." His condition had become so terrible that his associates were afraid to approach his bedside, and as he passed away, his nurse said that for all of the wealth in Europe, she would never watch another infidel die. A few years after he died the Geneva Bible Society purchased Voltaire's home and turned it into a print shop to print Bibles.*

Dietrich Bonhoffer, *German theologian, standing in front of a firing squad during World War 2, for speaking out against Nazism, "This may seem to be the end for me, but it is just the beginning."*

THOUGHT FOR THE DAY:
The death of a child of God is much different than the death of one who is lost and does not know Christ as their Savior. There is no hope in this world without Him.

CHRISTIANS NEVER SAY "GOOD-BYE" JUST "UNTIL WE MEET AGAIN"

DAY 22 – Heb. 11:22

Amplified: *[Actuated] by faith Joseph, when nearing the end of his life, referred to [the promise of God for] the departure of the Israelites out of Egypt and gave instructions concerning the burial of his own bones. (Amplified Bible - Lockman)*

KJV: *By faith Joseph, when he died, made mention of the departing of the children of Israel; and gave commandment concerning his bones.*

NLT: *And it was by faith that Joseph, when he was about to die, confidently spoke of God's bringing the people of Israel out of Egypt. He was so sure of it that he commanded them to carry his bones with them when they left! (NLT - Tyndale House)*

Phillips: *It was by faith that Joseph on his death-bed spoke of the exodus of the Israelites, and gave confident orders about the disposal of his own mortal remains. (Phillips: Touchstone)*

Wuest: *By faith Joseph, when coming near to the end of his life, remembered the exodus of the sons of Israel and so gave a command concerning his bones. (**Eerdmans**)*

Young's Literal: *by faith, Joseph dying, concerning the outgoing of the sons of Israel did make mention, and concerning his bones did give command.*

FROM MATTHEW HENRY

Now Joseph gave this order, not that he thought his being buried in Egypt would either prejudice his soul or prevent the resurrection of his body (as some of the rabbis fancied that all the Jews who were buried out of Canaan must be conveyed underground to Canaan before they could rise again), but to testify,

[1.] *That though he had lived and died in Egypt, yet he did not live and die an Egyptian, but an Israelite.*

[2.] *That he preferred a significant burial in Canaan before a magnificent one in Egypt.*

[3.] *That he would go as far with his people as he could, though he could not go as far as he would.*

[4.] *That he believed the resurrection of the body, and the communion that his soul should presently have with departed saints, as his body had with their dead bodies.*

[5.] *To assure them that God would be with them in Egypt, and deliver them out of it in his own time and way.*

THEY HAD SO LITTLE.

Warren Wiersbe makes the point that "We have to admire the faith of the patriarchs. They did not have a complete Bible, and yet their faith was strong. They handed God's promises down from one generation to another.

In spite of their failures and testings, these men and women believed God and He bore witness to their faith. How much more faith you and I should have!

PERSONAL QUESTION:

How are you showing to your family and friends your faith in God's promises?

_____
_____
_____
_____
_____
_____
_____

DAY 23 – Heb. 11:23

Amplified: [Prompted] by faith Moses, after his birth, was kept concealed for three months by his parents, because they saw how comely the child was; and they were not overawed and terrified by the king's decree. (*Amplified Bible - Lockman*)

KJV: By faith Moses, when he was born, was hid three months of his parents, because they saw he was a proper child; and they were not afraid of the king's commandment. (*NLT - Tyndale House*)

Phillips: It was by faith that Moses was hidden by his parents for three months after his birth, for they saw that he was an exceptional child and refused to be daunted by the king's decree that all male children should be drowned. (*Phillips: Touchstone*)

Wuest: By faith Moses, having been born, was hid three months by his parents, because they saw that he was a comely child. And they did not fear the mandate of the king. (*Eerdmans*)

Young's Literal: By faith Moses, having been born, was hid three months by his parents, because they saw the child comely, and were not afraid of the decree of the king

FAITHFUL PARENTS
Faith prompted the hiding of baby Moses, illustrating that genuine **faith** inspires noble conduct. One act of faith by God-fearing, God-trusting parents!

While they may have had an "inkling" that their son was destined for some divine duty ("he was beautiful" Ex 2:2, Acts 7:20), they could not have fully comprehended the bountiful fruit the sowing of their seeds of faith would one day bring forth for the entire nation of Israel and ultimately for the world!

Oh, how we all need to be reminded of the importance of remaining faithful in our daily lives. Only time will reveal what to us at the moment may have seemed like such a small act of faithful obedience and yet what God used to bring forth a bountiful harvest of righteousness. God give us all the grace to persevere in faithful obedience moment by moment, day by day, until our last breath opens the way into your glorious Presence.

APPLICATION

How can we apply the lessons from this godly example of faith?

(1) **Do not fear** *the Pharaohs in your life*
(Pr 29:25, Mt 10:28, Ps 25:15).

(2) **Entrust** *your children into God's watch care! And for all of you who were born into "Moses-like" godly homes where both parents were believers, let your praise and thanksgiving for such a wonderful gift continually resound to the Giver of all good gifts!* **(Jas 1:17)**

GREAT QUOTE ON PARENTS

Warren Wiersbe - *"Though godly parents cannot pass on their faith as they do family traits, they can certainly create an atmosphere of faith at home and be examples to their children. A home should be the first school of faith for a child."*

PERSONAL QUESTIONS

1. If you have children or grandchildren, what fears do you have for their future?

   _____
   _____
   _____
   _____
   _____
   _____

2. Why is it so hard to trust God with our children?

   _____
   _____
   _____

If you have children or grandchildren, pause now and pray for God's blessings and protection on their lives.

MOSES

DAY 24 – Heb. 11:24

Amplified: [Aroused] by faith Moses, when he had grown to maturity and become great, refused to be called the son of Pharaoh's daughter, (Amplified Bible - Lockman)

KJV: By faith Moses, when he was come to years, refused to be called the son of Pharaoh's daughter;

NLT: It was by faith that Moses, when he grew up, refused to be treated as the son of Pharaoh's daughter. (NLT - Tyndale House)

Phillips: It was also by faith that Moses himself when grown up refused to be called the son of Pharaoh's daughter. (Phillips: Touchstone)

Wuest: By faith Moses, when he had grown up, refused to be called a son of Pharaoh's daughter, (Eerdmans)

Young's Literal: by faith Moses, having become great, did refuse to be called a son of the daughter of Pharaoh,

MIGHTY MOSES

Moses the servant of God was a man of faith who used his eyes of faith (2Cor 5:7) to "see the invisible, to choose the imperishable (1Pe 1:4), and do the impossible (Ph. 4:13-note Lk 1:37).

What was true for Moses centuries ago can be true for all of God's children (He 11:6) today, but men and women of faith like Moses seem to be in short supply. Whatever our churches may be known for today, they're not especially known for glorifying God by great exploits of faith. Someone is recorded as jesting that "The church used to be known for its good deeds, but today it's better known for its bad mortgages."

THREE VICTORIES BY MOSES

*In **He 11:24, 25, 26** the writer gives us a very clear picture of temptation. Temptation can only come to a believer through three channels. These channels are (1) the lust of the flesh — what I want to do, (2) the lust of the eyes — what I want to have, and (3) the pride of life — what I want to be.*

When Moses chose to endure ill-treatment with the people of God, he faced and overcame the "lusts of the flesh" — what he wanted to do. He did this with the clear realization that he was choosing the eternal rather than the temporal and committing himself to the path of duty rather than to all the pleasures which may have been his in the palace of the king.

Secondly, when Moses reckoned the reproach of the Messiah a greater wealth than the treasures of Egypt, he overcame "the lust of the eyes" — what he wanted to have. Archaeologists have given us some idea of the wealth and treasure of Egypt.

Moses was perfectly conscious of what he was doing. He was turning his back on the "Fort Knox" of his day, and spurning all the influence and power which money could have obtained for him.

Thirdly, his faith and foresight helped him to set his mind upon future rewards and rise above any personal desires which he may have had for his own temporal advancement. In so doing he overcame the pride of life" — what he wanted to be.

What reason is given for these actions? The inspired writer attributes it solely to faith. By faith, Moses could see that the temporal things were going to pass away and that only that which was eternal would last. He overcame the temptation of selfish ambition, worldly pleasure and carnal possession because he did everything in life with a view to receiving God's approval. (**Moses A Study of Hebrews 1123-29a -- By Cyril J. Barber**)

What victories have you accomplished in your life by faith?

_____
_____
_____
_____
_____
_____

DAY 25 – Heb. 11:25

Amplified: *Because he preferred to share the oppression [suffer the hardships] and bear the shame of the people of God rather than to have the fleeting enjoyment of a sinful life. (Amplified Bible - Lockman)*

KJV: *Choosing rather to suffer affliction with the people of God, than to enjoy the pleasures of sin for a season;*

NLT: *He chose to share the oppression of God's people instead of enjoying the fleeting pleasures of sin. (NLT - Tyndale House)*

Phillips: *He preferred sharing the burden of God's people to enjoying the temporary advantages of alliance with a sinful nation. (Phillips: Touchstone)*

Wuest: *having chosen for himself rather to be suffering affliction with the people of God than to be having sin's enjoyments temporarily (**Eerdmans**)*

Young's Literal: *having chosen rather to be afflicted with the people of God, than to have sin's pleasure for a season,*

GREAT COMMENTS on MOSES

Spurgeon - *He perceived the pleasures of sin to be but for a season. He said to himself, "I may have but a short time to live, and even if I live to a good old age, life at the longest is still short. When I come to the close of life, what a miserable reflection it will be that I have had all my pleasure, it is all over, and now I have to appear before God as a traitorous*

Israelite who threw up his birthright for the sake of enjoying the pleasures of Egypt."

Warren Wiersbe - *As with Abraham and Moses of old, the decisions we make today will determine the rewards tomorrow. More than this, our decisions should be motivated by the expectation of receiving rewards (Ed: which is clearly what motivated Moses' decision to defer)...The emphasis in the Epistle to the Hebrews is: 'Don't live for what the world will promise you today! Live for what God has promised you in the future!"*

GREAT EXAMPLES BY JESUS

Jesus *present two powerful examples of any who would seek to enjoy the passing pleasures of what this world has to offer...*

Luke 12:19 *(Parable of a certain rich man who says) 'And I will say to my soul, "Soul, you have many goods laid up for many years to come; take your ease, eat, drink and be merry."' 20 "But God said to him, 'You fool! This very night your soul is required of you; and now who will own what you have prepared?'*

Disciple's Study Bible *comments that "The present is not permanent. People make plans for the future based on present achievements. Such plans should not be totally self-centered. We need to remember God controls the future. Our plans must include Him, His will, and His work on earth. Our largest building project is His kingdom.*

Luke 16:25 *- "But Abraham said (to the rich man, 'Child, remember that during your life you received your good things, and likewise Lazarus bad things; but now he is being comforted here, and you are in agony.*

"PLEASURES OF SIN FOR A SEASON"

Moses perceived the pleasures of sin to be but for a season. He said to himself, "I may have but a short time to live, and even if I live to a good old age, life at the longest is still short. When I come to the close of life, what a miserable reflection it will be that I have had all my pleasure, it is all over, and now I have to appear before God as one who threw up his birthright for the sake of enjoying the pleasures of Egypt."

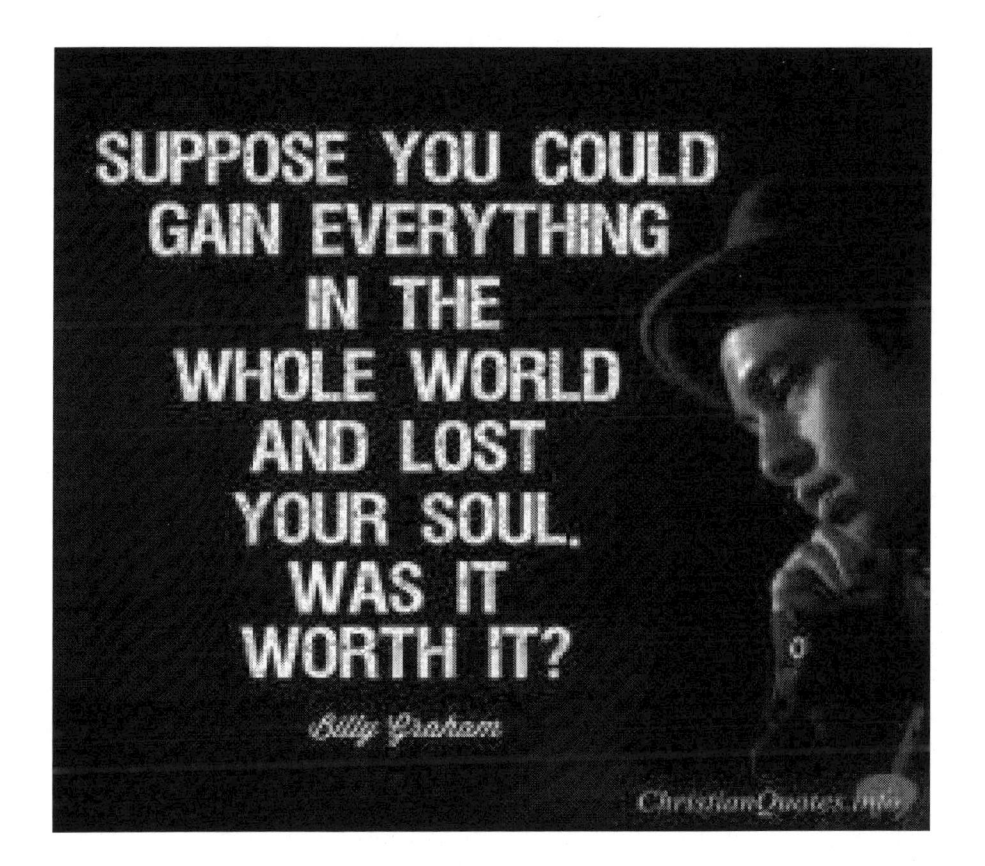

DAY 26 – Heb. 11:26

Amplified: He considered the contempt and abuse and shame [borne for] the Christ (the Messiah Who was to come) to be greater wealth than all the treasures of Egypt, for he looked forward and away to the reward (recompense). (<u>Amplified Bible - Lockman</u>)

KJV: Esteeming the reproach of Christ greater riches than the treasures in Egypt: for he had respect unto the recompence of the reward.

NLT: He thought it was better to suffer for the sake of the Messiah than to own the treasures of Egypt, for he was looking ahead to the great reward that God would give him. (<u>NLT - Tyndale House</u>)

Phillips: He considered the "reproach of Christ" more precious than all the wealth of Egypt, for he looked steadily at the ultimate, not the immediate, reward. By faith he led the exodus from Egypt; he defied the king's anger with the strength that came from obedience to the invisible king. (<u>Phillips: Touchstone</u>)

Wuest: he considered the reproach of the Messiah greater wealth than Egypt's treasures, for he looked away to the recompense. (<u>Eerdmans</u>)

Young's Literal: having chosen rather to be afflicted with the people of God, than to have sin's pleasure for a season,

GREAT THOUGHTS

***Henry Morris** on the "**Reproaches of Christ**"*
*Moses lived about 1500 years before Christ, but even at this early date, he knew about the promised Messiah (see, for example, his prophecy in <u>Deuteronomy 18:15-19</u>), and knew God's eternal promises to Abraham, Isaac and Jacob were worth far more than temporal riches. (**<u>Defender's Study Bible</u>**)*

***Wiersbe** makes a good point that "God always rewards true faith—if not immediately, at least ultimately. Over against "the treasures in Egypt" Moses saw the "recompense of the reward."*

Dr. Vance Havner said, "Moses chose the imperishable, saw the invisible, and did the impossible." (<u>Wiersbe, W: Bible Exposition Commentary. 1989. Victor</u>)

A DEAD CHURCH

***John MacArthur** tells story - 'There once was an old church in England. A sign on the front of the building read "**We preach Christ crucified**." After a time, ivy grew up and obscured the last word..."**We preach Christ.**" The ivy grew some more, and motto read, "**We preach.**" Finally, ivy covered the entire sign, and the church died. Such is the fate of any church that fails to* *carry out its mission in the world." The church continued and was later the scene of a major church council, but after the 5th century both the church and the city declined. The immediate area has been uninhabited since the 14th century.*

**O Lord, return to me Your power
That once by grace I knew;
Forgive the sin that grieved Your heart,
And help me to be true.
--Anon.**

CHOICES IN LIFE

We all have to make choices in life, and often those choices result in significant consequences. In 1920, the management of the Boston Red Sox made the bad choice to sell Babe Ruth to the New York Yankees. After joining the Yankees, in 10 out of the next 12 seasons Ruth hit more home runs than the entire Red Sox team! Boston had not won a World Series since 1918, when Ruth was on the team, until this week!

In 1938, Joe Schuster and Jerry Siegel sold all their rights for a comic book character that they had invented for $130. The character's name? Superman! In 1955, Sam Phillips sold to RCA Victor Records his exclusive contract with a young singer named Elvis Presley, thus forfeiting royalties on more than a billion records (Reader's Digest [7/85], p. 173). Bad choices!

Our text tells us about two good choices that greatly affected world history. The first choice was relatively routine at the time. Two slaves in ancient Egypt chose to defy the king's edict to kill all male Hebrew babies by hiding their son. That son turned out to be Moses, the great deliverer of his people. The second choice was that of Moses himself, and it was more difficult. He chose to give up his position of influence and wealth in the Egyptian court in order to side with the enslaved people of God. Both choices were motivated by faith and their lessons have eternal consequences for us.

PERSONAL QUESTIONS

How would you answer someone who said, "I want to enjoy the things of this world for a while; then I'll trust in Christ"?

_____
_____
_____
_____
_____
_____
_____
_____
_____
_____
_____

How can we keep the greater riches of Christ in view when the world's treasures parade by us daily?

_____
_____
_____
_____

When is it right to defy governmental or parental authority?

_____
_____
_____
_____
_____

Could Moses have had more influence by remaining in Pharaoh's court?

_____
_____
_____
_____
_____
_____

When is it time to separate from worldly friends?

_____
_____
_____
_____
_____
_____
_____
_____

DAY 27 – Heb. 11:27

Amplified: [Motivated] by faith he left Egypt behind him, being unawed and undismayed by the wrath of the king; for he never flinched but held staunchly to his purpose and endured steadfastly as one who gazed on Him Who is invisible.

KJV: By faith he forsook Egypt, not fearing the wrath of the king: for he endured, as seeing him who is invisible.

NLT: It was by faith that Moses left the land of Egypt. He was not afraid of the king. Moses kept right on going because he kept his eyes on the one who is invisible. (NLT - Tyndale House)

McGee - Moses had faith to act—faith will lead to action. Many folk today are saying, "I believe, I believe," but do nothing. May I say, faith reveals itself in action. God saves us without our works, but the faith that saves produces works. Therefore Moses "forsook Egypt, not fearing the wrath of the king: for he endured, as seeing him who is invisible."

MacDonald – Moses feared Pharaoh so little because he feared God so much. He kept his eyes on "the blessed and only Potentate, the King of kings and Lord of lords, who alone has immortality, dwelling in unapproachable light, whom no man has seen or can see, to whom be honor and everlasting power. Amen" (1Ti 6:15, 16). (MacDonald, W & Farstad, A. Believer's Bible Commentary: Thomas Nelson)

APPLICATION

*These passages in Hebrews 11also give us a sense of how we as believers should "leave" the world (to be sure we are to be "**in** the world" but we not to be **of** the world). We are to "leave our garments" so to speak every time the world seeks to arrest our attention! We are to get out, not looking back as did Lot's wife, who became a pillar of salt! (Lk 17:32, 33, Ge 19:28, cp 1Co 6:18-note , Jude 1:23).*

We are to make it our lifestyle like Joseph to continually flee youthful lusts (2Ti 2:22 - where "flee" is present imperative). When temptation attacks our mind (as when Potiphar's wife tempted Joseph) we are to have the attitude of the popular Nike commercial which says ''Just do it!" "Leave Egypt!"

*The **NLT** paraphrases it this way "Moses kept right on going because he kept his eyes on the one who is invisible."*

***Richard Phillips** records - A great Christian example comes from the Scottish Reformer John Knox. When asked how he could so boldly confront the Roman Catholic queen, Knox replied, "One does not fear the Queen of Scotland when he has been on his knees before the King of Kings." It is said that Napoleon would sometimes call his generals in one by one before a great battle to gaze on them without speaking and let them look upon his face. In a similar way, the man or woman of frequent communion with God in prayer and in his Word will see His face in the midst of the fight, thereby finding courage and a strong incentive to faith. (Reformed Expository Commentary – Hebrews)*

From Hebrews 11:27, here are three obstacles that faith must overcome:

> *(1)* **Faith** *often puts us into opposition with powerful forces.*
>
> *(2)* **Faith** *enables us to obey God without fear.*
>
> *(3)* **Faith** *overcomes powerful opposition by seeing the unseen God.*

PERSONAL QUESTION

After 27 days of your journey of faith, describe where your faith status today. Be honest with yourself.

_____
_____
_____
_____
_____
_____

GOD HAS A **PURPOSE** BEHIND EVERY PROBLEM

Rick Warren

ChristianQuotes.info

DAY 28 – Heb. 11:28

NLT: *It was by faith that Moses commanded the people of Israel to keep the Passover and to sprinkle blood on the doorposts so that the angel of death would not kill their firstborn sons.*

Phillips: *By faith Moses kept the first Passover and made the blood-sprinkling, so that the angel of death which killed the first-born should not touch his people. (Phillips: Touchstone)*

Wuest: *By faith he instituted the Passover and the sprinkling of the blood in order that the destroyer of the first-born should not touch them. (**Eerdmans**)*

Wiersbe - **Faith** *in the Word led to the Passover deliverance (how the Egyptians must have scoffed at the blood on the doors!) and the crossing of the Red Sea. (Wiersbe, W. W. Wiersbe's Expository Outlines on the New Testament. Wheaton, Ill.: Victor Books)*

The Blood of the Lamb kept the Jews unhurt in the midst of the Egyptians and in the presence of so great a destruction, and much more will the blood of Christ save us, for whom it has been sprinkled not on our doorposts but in our souls. For even now the destroyer is still moving around in the depth of night; but let us be armed with Christ's sacrifice, since God has brought us out from Egypt, from darkness and from idolatry."

Illustration - *The story is told of one who, passing through a village in Basutoland, noticed some chickens with little red ribbons fastened to their backs between their wings. The people explained: "They protect the chickens from the many vicious hawks that otherwise would attack them. The hawks are afraid of red ribbons. Neither blue, nor green nor any other color would provide the needed immunity from attack." Are we eternally tied by the red ribbon of the atoning blood? "*

FAITH THAT FEARS NO CANNIBALS!

John G. Paton *(1824-1907), who left his native Scotland to take the gospel to the cannibals of the New Hebrides Islands, answers that question well. As he was getting ready to leave, an elderly friend repeatedly sought to deter him. His crowning argument was always, "The Cannibals! You will be eaten by Cannibals!"* (**You Will Be Eaten by Cannibals! Lessons from the Life of John G. Paton from Dr John Piper - if you have time listen to the Mp3**)

Paton *finally replied,*

Mr. Dickson, you are advanced in years now, and your own prospect is to be soon laid in the grave, there to be eaten by worms. I confess to you, that if I can but live and die serving and honoring the Lord Jesus, it will make no difference to me whether I am eaten by Cannibals or worms. And in the Great Day my resurrection body will arise as fair as yours in the likeness of our risen Redeemer" (John G. Paton Autobiography [Banner of Truth], p. 56).

Let's join **Paton** *and* **Moses** *as people of over-coming faith, who endure by seeing the unseen God!*

PERSONAL QUESTIONS

Why is it important for Christians to expect opposition and hardship? Why do many naively think that the Christian life will be trouble-free?

What are your biggest personal fears? How can we overcome our fears?

Someone says, "Many Christians have trusted God and have been killed, not delivered. Why should I trust in such a God?" How would you answer?

_____
_____
_____
_____
_____
_____
_____
_____
_____
_____
_____
_____
_____
_____
_____
_____
_____
_____
_____
_____
_____

DAY 29 – Heb. 11:29

NLT: *It was by faith that the people of Israel went right through the Red Sea as though they were on dry ground. But when the Egyptians followed, they were all drowned. (NLT - Tyndale House)*

Phillips: *By faith the people walked through the Red Sea as though it were dry land, and the Egyptians who tried to do the same thing were drowned. (Phillips: Touchstone)*

Faith is believing that God will keep His promises, despite circumstances that seem to be to the contrary! True faith that saves one's soul includes at least three main elements - (1) firm persuasion or firm conviction, (2) a surrender to that truth and (3) a conduct emanating from that surrender. In sum, faith shows itself genuine by a changed life.

GREAT POINT!

Guzik – *"The difference between the Israelites crossing the Red Sea and the Egyptians who followed them was not courage, but faith. The Egyptians had as much (or more) courage than the Israelites, but not the same faith - and they each had different fates. The Israelites passed through, and the Egyptians were drowned."*

Steven Cole in his sermon on **Overcoming Faith** writes...

1. Faith does not exempt us from overwhelming problems, but rather it often leads us into such problems.

If Israel had stayed in Egypt, they wouldn't be in the mess they were in at the Red Sea. So by God's direct actions, this defenseless bunch of slaves had the Red Sea in front of them and Pharaoh's army charging at them from behind. They were doomed unless God intervened, which He planned to do. But they had to learn that salvation is completely from Him. There was no place for human ingenuity or some scheme to escape. God led them into this desperate situation to teach them to trust Him as their only option.

That's how God grows our faith. We know in our heads that we must trust Him totally, but we don't believe it in practice until He throws us into situations where there is no way out if He does not act. We need to learn in experience that "salvation belong

2. God delights to turn our overwhelming problems into exhibitions of His mighty power when we trust Him.

The situation that the enemy thought would bring them an easy victory led to their defeat. God miraculously piled the water up as a wall on both sides for Israel to walk through on dry ground (Ex 14:21, 22). He moved the pillar of cloud behind them until they all passed through.

Then He let the Egyptians pursue them in blind fury. And so a helpless, defenseless, unorganized band of two million slaves were delivered from a powerful, well-equipped army. Nothing is too difficult for the Lord (Jer 32:17)!

PERSONAL QUESTIONS

What are you facing today that is overwhelming to you?

_____
_____
_____
_____
_____
_____
_____

Do you believe God will keep His promises and lead you through this to victory?

_____
_____
_____
_____
_____
_____
_____
_____
_____
_____
_____
_____
_____
_____

Moses at the Red Sea

DAY 30 – Heb. 11:30

Phillips: *It was by faith that the walls of Jericho collapsed, for the people had obeyed God's command to encircle them for seven days. (Phillips: Touchstone)*

Wuest: *By faith the walls of Jericho fell, having been encircled seven days. (**Eerdmans**)*

Young's Literal: *by faith the walls of Jericho did fall, having been surrounded for seven days;*

JERICHO

Jericho like the Red Sea presented an obstacle to Israel. We need to remember that obstacles to us are "opportunities" for God to show Himself great and mighty in our life.

Here is the account of this great God glorifying event from Joshua 6:

1 Now Jericho was tightly shut because of the sons of Israel; no one went out and no one came in.

2 The LORD said to Joshua, "See, **I have given Jericho into your hand**, with its king and the valiant warriors. 3 "You shall march around the city, all the men of war circling the city once. You shall do so for six days. 4 "Also seven priests shall carry seven trumpets of rams' horns before the ark; then on the seventh day you shall march around the city seven times, and the priests shall blow the trumpets. 5 "It shall be that when they make a long blast with the ram's horn, and when you hear the sound of the trumpet, all the people shall shout with a great

shout; and the wall of the city will fall down flat, and the people will go up every man straight ahead."
6 So Joshua the son of Nun called the priests and said to them, "Take up the ark of the covenant, and let seven priests carry seven trumpets of rams' horns before the ark of the LORD." 7 Then he said to the people, "Go forward, and march around the city, and let the armed men go on before the ark of the LORD."

The walls of Jericho fell down - *Liberal scholars try to explain away this supernatural intervention, but faith sees it as a clear indicator of God's mighty power at work on the part of His people.* **We need to remember that He is the same mighty God in each of our lives.**

What are the insurmountable walls in your life?

_____
_____
_____
_____
_____
_____

LESSONS LEARNED

Many great lessons of faith are gleaned from Israel's march around Jericho.

1) *God's way of victory over these enemies accentuates His power and our weakness.*

2) ***Faith*** *must obey God implicitly.*

3) ***Faith*** *must wait upon God.*

4) ***Faith*** *must wait on God expectantly.*

FAITH & OBEDIENCE

Believing and obeying always run side by side...Faith and obedience are bound up in the same bundle. He that obeys God, trusts God; and he that trusts God, obeys God. In short, obedience is the hallmark of faith.

PRAYER

Pray today that God will increase your faith and give you the ability to believe Him for greater things in ministry to others than you have ever seen. Maybe God will send someone to you today who needs help and they will be depending on your faith because they are weak. Pray for God to prepare your heart now.

Joshua at Jericho

DAY 31 – Heb. 11:31

Wuest: *By faith Rahab the harlot did not perish with those who were disobedient, having received the spies with peace. (<u>Eerdmans</u>)*

Young's Literal: *by faith Rahab the harlot did not perish with those who disbelieved, having received the spies with peace.*

ABOUT RAHAB

W.E. Vine writes that *"Rahab had a simple faith and very elementary, but it was real. She knew what God had determined, and acted accordingly. She grasped the unseen, and put her belief into action. Hence her life was lifted out from the influences of her lost condition, and her faith brought her from her alienated state into the fellowship of God's people.* (<u>Vine, W. Collected writings of W. E. Vine. Nashville: Thomas Nelson</u>)

RAHAB THE.....HARLOT.

Scripture is brutally honest. Yes, she became <u>**Rahab**</u> the believer, but the Scripture reminds us of how God is able to take us from the **"guttermost"** and lift us to the **"uttermost"**, from eternal death to eternal life, independent of how evil we were before we entered into His great salvation **by faith**. In summary, Rahab was saved by God's grace and by her personal faith which was shown to be genuine by her good works of preserving the life of the spies.

***William Newell** n*otes the following seven points about Rahab's life and faith"

1. Rahab was a common sinner, even a harlot. God says as to all of us. "There is no difference; for all have sinned."

2. Rehab's faith (Josh. 2:8–11) was confessed by her in the words, "I know that Jehovah hath given you the land, and that the fear of you is fallen upon us, and that all the inhabitants of the land melt away before you."

3. This belief meant complete turning against her own people, just as a believer now comes out from, and is no longer of, the world.

4. It included belief that Jericho would be destroyed (Josh 2:13); and it brought concern for her own kin.

5. It brought about the beautiful typical picture of the scarlet cord, tied up in her window, by which the spies also escaped (Josh 2:15–21). How that cord reminds us of the shed blood of Christ!

6. By her faith she, her father, her mother, her brethren, and all her kindred—"Whosoever shall be with thee in the house"—(Josh 2:19), were preserved (Josh 6:22–23, 25).

7. She became the mother of Boaz (Matt. 1:5), great-grandfather of David the king! (Ruth 4:21–2).

NO MORE EXCUSES

The exercise of **faith** by **Rahab the harlot** brought her not only salvation, but into the line of the Messiah for she was the mother of godly Boaz, a man who in many ways pictured the "Greater Boaz", Christ Jesus.

Imagine a pagan harlot becoming a part of the ancestry of Jesus Christ! That is what faith can do! Rahab is certainly a rebuke to unsaved people who give excuses for not trusting Christ.

"I don't know very much about the Bible" is an excuse I often hear. Rahab knew very little spiritual truth, but she acted on what she did know.

"I am too bad to be saved!" is another excuse. But Rahab was a condemned heathen harlot! Another excuse is,

"What will my family think?" Rahab's first concern was saving her family, not opposing them. She stands as one of the great women of faith in the Bible.

PERSONAL QUESTIONS

Why doesn't God grant instant deliverance from our problems? Why do some problems linger on for years?

_____
_____
_____

How can we get faith when we lack faith? Where is the heart of the problem of unbelief?

Many sinners want to clean up their lives before they can be saved. Is that necessary to come to Christ?

Rahab the Harlot

DAY 32 – Heb. 11:32

KJV: And what shall I more say? for the time would fail me to tell of Gedeon, and of Barak, and of Samson, and of Jephthae; of David also, and Samuel, and of the prophets:

NLT: Well, how much more do I need to say? It would take too long to recount the stories of the faith of Gideon, Barak, Samson, Jephthah, David, Samuel, and all the prophets. (NLT - Tyndale House)

STUDYING THE TEXT

"Time will fail me" – *Why does time fail the writer of Hebrews? He had so many OT examples of faith that he could have given to encourage his Hebrew readers. However, he was running out of time, not examples of faithful men and women.*

Gideon, Barak, Samson, Jephthah- *These 4 names come from one of the darkest times of Israel's history, the days of the Judges, which is tragically summed up by the declaration in Judges 21:25.*

Gideon *by faith defeated the Midianite army with a small band of 300 men. (see Judges 6-8)*

By faith **Barak** *with the prodding of Deborah was used by God to defeat the Canaanites. (see Judges 4, 5)*

Samson *defeated the Philistines several times most notably in his last act of faith in which he himself was killed.*

Jephthah *defeated the Ammonites with God's power (see Judges 11, 12)*

SPURGEON ON SAMSON

There are some names in this chapter that we should hardly have expected to see there, the characters mentioned having been so disfigured by serious faults, and flaws, and failings. But the distinguishing feature of faith was there in every instance, especially in the case of Samson. Perhaps there was no more childlike faith in any man than there was in him. Who but a man full of faith would have hurled himself upon a thousand men with no weapon in his hand but the jawbone of a donkey? There was a wondrous confidence in God in that weak, strong man, which, though it does not excuse his faults, yet nevertheless puts him in the ranks of the believers. Happy is the man or woman who believes in God.

The interesting thing is that the first five men all had some serious shortcomings, but in spite of these flaws, God honored their faith.

Gideon *at first was cowardly and had to be coaxed to do what God called him to do. After his amazing victory with 300 men over the Midianite army of 135,000, he made an ephod that lured Israel into idolatry (Judges 8:24, 25, 26, 27). Yet in spite of his failures, the author names him as a hero of faith.*

Barak *won a great victory for Israel over an army that had 900 chariots, but he only did it at the prodding of a woman, Deborah.*

Samson routed the Philistines on numerous occasions, yet he was tripped up by his lust for foreign women.

Jephthah, the son of a harlot, was at first driven away by his half-brothers. But later, the elders of his home town pled with him to return and lead them in battle against the enemy. He won a victory, but then made a rash vow to sacrifice the first thing that came out of his house when he returned from battle. His only daughter came out to greet him, and he foolishly kept his stupid vow.

David was a man after God's heart (Acts 13:22), who had great faith even as a teenager, when he defeated Goliath. But he later committed adultery and then murder to cover his tracks. Even Samuel, al-though a godly man himself, failed to raise his sons to follow the Lord (1Sa 8:1-23).

GOD USES BROKEN VESSELS.

William Carey, "the father of modern missions," had an illiterate wife who defiantly refused to go to India with him. He was going to go without her, but his departure was delayed by some problems.

He and his traveling companion returned to his house, where his companion laid a guilt trip on Carey's wife.
He warned her that if she didn't accompany them, her family "would be dispersed and divided forever and she would regret it as long as she lived" (Mary Drewery, Wiliam Carey [Zondervan], p. 52).

She fearfully went with them, only to be bitterly unhappy and finally to go insane in India. In addition, Carey himself was an overly indulgent father who did not correct his children (Ruth Tucker, From Jerusalem to Irian Jaya [Zondervan], p. 119).

Yet, God used William Carey in an extraordinary way through world-wide missions as few in history . The miracle is how God uses broken vessels for His glory. There is hope for you and me!!!

PERSONAL QUESTIONS

Do you ever doubt that God can use you because of weakness in your life?

_____
_____
_____
_____
_____
_____
_____

Samson

DAY 33 – Heb. 11:33

NLT: *By faith these people overthrew kingdoms, ruled with justice, and received what God had promised them. They shut the mouths of lions, (NLT - Tyndale House)*

Phillips: *Through their faith these men conquered kingdoms, ruled in justice and proved the truth of God's promises. They shut the mouths of lions, (Phillips: Touchstone)*

DANIEL and THE BIG CATS

"Shut the mouths of lions"- *This is a clear reference to the prophet Daniel in the lion's den because of failing to obey a pagan order not to pray to God. Daniel records the story in chapter 6:*

And when he (King Darius) had come near the den to Daniel, he cried out with a troubled voice. The king spoke and said to Daniel, "Daniel, servant of the living God, has your God, whom you constantly serve, been able to deliver you from the lions?" 21 Then Daniel spoke to the king, "O king, live forever! **22 "My God sent His angel and shut the lions' mouths, and they have not harmed me**, *inasmuch as I was found innocent before Him; and also toward you, O king, I have committed no crime." 23 Then the king was very pleased and gave orders for Daniel to be taken up out of the den. So Daniel was taken up out of the den, and no injury whatever was found on him, because he had trusted in his God. (Da 6:20, 21, 22, 23)*

Remember Daniel in the lions' den, and then ask yourself, "What is there that faith cannot do?"

How does this apply to believers in Christ today who are unlikely to be thrown into a literal lion's den? While a literal lion was Daniel's enemy, a **figurative lion** is our relentless ferocious foe, the <u>Devil</u> himself (and his minions) who ever seeks to "kill and destroy" our faith and our testimony for Jesus Christ. **Peter** writes that in order to **"shut the mouth"** of this **roaring lion** we must do the following:

*Be of sober spirit, be on the alert. (Both of these commands are **<u>aorist imperative</u>** in Greek = Do this now! Don't delay! Conveys a sense of urgency!) Your adversary, the **devil** (**<u>diabolos</u>**), prowls about **like a roaring lion**, (<u>2 Ti 4:17</u>, <u>18</u>) seeking someone to devour. But **resist** (also **<u>aorist imperative</u>**) him, firm in your faith, knowing that the same experiences of suffering are being accomplished by your brethren who are in the world. (<u>1Pe 5:8,</u> <u>1Pe 5:9</u>)*

PERSONAL QUESTIONS

What area of your life has Satan been attacking you lately?

_____
_____
_____

_____
_____
_____
_____
_____
_____
_____

Study Ephesians 6:111-18 and list the weapons you have in your battle against the Enemy of your soul!

_____
_____
_____
_____
_____
_____
_____
_____
_____
_____
_____
_____
_____
_____
_____
_____
_____

PRAYER FOR PUTTING ON THE ARMOR OF GOD EACH DAY

I recently led a series on Ephesians chapter 6 and taught about how to put on the armor of God each day. This is a prayer that was placed on my heart during that teaching series. I pray that it will be a blessing to your life. Use it and share it freely.

Good morning, Lord. It's going to be a great day because I am preparing to win spiritual battles for Your glory and honor! Your Word tells me to "Put on the armor of God that I may be able to stand against the schemes of the Devil" (Ephesians 6:12). So, I am here today dressing myself for battle.

I will buckle the truth of Your Word like a belt around me. I will speak the truth, live the truth and compare everything I hear today by the standards of Your Word, which is absolute truth.

I will strap on the breastplate of righteousness and ask You to let nothing into my heart today that You do not approve.

I will lace up the boots of readiness for sharing the Gospel of peace with those who do not know You. I am ready to tell others how to find You when I get the opportunity.

I will firmly hold on to the shield of faith and defeat every fiery dart of the Devil. I break every evil assignment against me in Jesus' Name!

I will confidently wear the helmet of salvation and ask You to keep my mind focused on things that are good, positive, pure and Christ-like.

I will take the sword of the Spirit, which is the Word of God, and stand on Your promises today when the enemy comes in like a flood, knowing that greater is He who is in me than he who is in the world.

I will pray without ceasing today in Your Spirit and look for opportunities to pray for those around me who are hurting and need You.

I am covered in the Blood of Jesus.
I am filled and anointed with the Holy Spirit.
I am protected by an army of angels.
I am loved by my Father in Heaven.

Look out, Satan……..it's going to be a bad day for you!

In Jesus' Name, Amen.

- Larry Petton

Daniel in the Lions' Den

DAY 34 – Heb. 11:34

Amplified: Extinguished the power of raging fire, escaped the devourings of the sword, out of frailty and weakness won strength and became stalwart, even mighty and resistless in battle, routing alien hosts. (Amplified Bible - Lockman)

KJV: Quenched the violence of fire, escaped the edge of the sword, out of weakness were made strong, waxed valiant in fight, turned to flight the armies of the aliens.

NLT: quenched the flames of fire, and escaped death by the edge of the sword. Their weakness was turned to strength. They became strong in battle and put whole armies to flight. (NLT - Tyndale House)

Phillips: they quenched the furious blaze of fire, they escaped from death itself. From being weaklings they became strong men and mighty warriors; they routed whole armies of foreigners. (Phillips: Touchstone)

Wuest: quenched the power of fire, escaped the edge of the sword, from weakness were made strong, became mighty in war, turned to flight armies of aliens.

Young's Literal: quenched the power of fire, escaped the mouth of the sword, were made powerful out of infirmities, became strong in battle, caused to give way camps of the aliens.

Shadrach, Meshach and Abednego *are the obvious examples of this manifestation of faith in verse 34. Their story of faith is found in Daniel chapter 3.*

DANIEL 3

*Then Nebuchadnezzar was filled with wrath, and his facial expression was altered toward Shadrach, Meshach and Abed-nego. He answered by giving orders to heat the furnace seven times more than it was usually heated. 20 And he commanded certain valiant warriors who were in his army to tie up Shadrach, Meshach and Abed-nego, in order to cast them into the furnace of blazing fire. 21 Then these men were tied up in their trousers, their coats, their caps and their other clothes, and were cast into the midst of the furnace of blazing fire. (See notes on **Daniel 3:19, 20, 21**)*

*While the writer doubtless refers to quenching **the power** of literal **fire**, there is an application to all believers in Christ of all generations.*

*The **Psalmist** records the faithfulness of God in the fire: "You made men ride over our heads; We went through fire and through water, Yet You brought us out into a place of abundance." (Ps 66:12)*

Through Isaiah God promised…"When you pass through the waters, I will be with you; and through the rivers, they will not overflow you.

When you walk through the fire, you will not be scorched, nor will the flame burn you" (Isaiah 43:2).

Would you like to do something great for God? Have you heard the motto of our early missionaries,

"Attempt great things for God"?

Does that thought burn within your heart? Do you long to be of some great use? "Oh, yes," says one, "I would attempt great things for God, but I am terribly weak." Make the attempt by faith in God, for it is written about people "who through faith subdued kingdoms, worked righteousness, obtained promises, stopped the mouths of lions, quenched the violence of fire, escaped the edge of the sword, out of weakness were made strong, became valiant in battle, turned to flight the armies of the aliens" (Heb. 11:33, 34).

If you feel incapable, throw yourself on the infinite capacity of God. As long as you are willing to be used, as long as God has given you a concern and a labor of spirit for the souls of others, you need not fear. You may by faith get to work in all your feebleness, for "as your days so shall your strength be" (Dt 33:25). Has not the Lord said to you, "My grace is sufficient for you, for My strength is made perfect in weakness" (2Cor. 12:9).

My dear friend, Raelene Hudson*, loves the Lord with all of her heart and is a blessing to everyone she meets. She believes God for big things for our church and her life. She once shared an acronym of BIG faith with me that I loved! It's pretty simple.*

B-elieve
I-n
G-od

PERSONAL CHALLENGE!!

Would you stop right now and ask God to give you a BIG faith today so that you can move mountains that stand in your way!

DAY 35 – Heb. 11:35

Amplified: *[Some] women received again their dead by a resurrection. Others were tortured to death with clubs, refusing to accept release [offered on the terms of denying their faith], so that they might be resurrected to a better life. (Amplified Bible - Lockman)*

KJV: *Women received their dead raised to life again: and others were tortured, not accepting deliverance; that they might obtain a better resurrection:*

NLT: *Women received their loved ones back again from death. But others trusted God and were tortured, preferring to die rather than turn from God and be free. They placed their hope in the resurrection to a better life. (NLT - Tyndale House)*

Phillips: *Some returned to their womenfolk from certain death, while others were tortured and refused to be ransomed, because they wanted to deserve a more honourable resurrection in the world to come. (Phillips: Touchstone)*

Wuest: *Women received by resurrection their dead, and others were tortured, not accepting the deliverance in order that they might obtain a better resurrection. (Eerdmans)*

Young's Literal: *Women received by a rising again their dead, and others were tortured, not accepting the redemption, that a better rising again they might receive,*

JOHN WYCLIFFE *(1329-1384) English reformer; Bible translator - A native of Yorkshire, Wycliffe attended Oxford University, where he received a doctorate of theology in 1372.*

Wycliffe, the most eminent Oxford theologian of his day, and his associates, were the first to translate the entire Bible from Latin into English. His teachings influenced John HUS and laid the foundations for the PROTESTANT REFORMATION on the Continent.

Wycliffe has been called the "MORNING STAR OF THE REFORMATION" because he boldly questioned papal authority, criticized the sale of indulgences (which were supposed to release a person from punishment in purgatory), denied the reality of transubstantiation (the doctrine that the bread and wine are changed into Jesus Christ's actual body and blood during Communion), and spoke out against church hierarchies. The pope reproved Wycliffe for his heretical teachings and asked that Oxford University dismiss him. But Oxford and many government leaders stood with Wycliffe, so he was able to survive the pope's assaults.

***Wycliffe believed that the way to prevail in his struggle with the church's abusive authority was to make the Bible available to the people in their own language. Then they could read for themselves how each one of them could have a personal relationship with God through Jesus Christ**—apart from any ecclesiastical authority. Wycliffe, with his associates, completed the New Testament around 1380 and the Old Testament in 1382. Wycliffe concentrated his labors on the New Testament, while an associate, Nicholas of Hereford, did a major part of the Old Testament. Wycliffe and his coworkers, unfamiliar with the original Hebrew and Greek, translated the Latin text into English. Therefore, their Bible was a translation of a translation, not a translation of the original languages. With the coming of the Renaissance came the resurgence of the study of the classics—and with it the resurgence of the study of Greek, as well as Hebrew.*

Thus, for the first time in nearly a thousand years (500–1500—the approximate time when Latin was the dominant language for scholarship, except in the Greek church) scholars began to read the New Testament in its original language, Greek. By 1500, Greek was being taught at Oxford.

After Wycliffe finished the translation work, he organized a group of poor parishioners, known as __Lollards__, to go throughout England preaching Christian truths and reading the Scriptures in their mother tongue to all who would hear God's word. As a result the Word of God, through Wycliffe's translation, became available to many Englishmen.

Wycliffe was loved and hated. *His ecclesiastical enemies did not forget his opposition to their power or his successful efforts in making the Scriptures available to all. Several decades after he died they condemned him for heresy, dug up his body, burned it, and threw his ashes into the Swift River.*

If you enjoy reading your Bible today…..you can thank God for using a man of fearless faith like John Wycliffe!

PERSONAL QUESTIONS

Have you ever been hated for your faith in Jesus Christ?

_____
_____
_____
_____
_____
_____

Wycliffe gave his life and risked everything so we could have a copy of God's Word in our hands. How much does your Bible mean to you? How much time do you spend in an average week in reading the Scripture?

_____
_____
_____
_____
_____
_____
_____
_____

DAY 36 - Heb. 11:36

KJV: And others had trial of cruel mockings and scourgings, yea, moreover of bonds and imprisonment:

NLT: Some were mocked, and their backs were cut open with whips. Others were chained in dungeons. (NLT - Tyndale House)

Phillips: Others were exposed to the test of public mockery and flogging, and to the torture of being left bound in prison.

"MOCKINGS" (empaigmos from empaizo = to mock) includes the ideas of scoffing, derisive contemptuous remarks, public ridicule. While we might all agree that mocking is better than the torture rack, we need to be honest and acknowledge that this genre of suffering for our faith is very painful to our soul, and especially so when it comes from those who are (or were) close to us, such as friends and family.

EXAMPLES OF MOCKERY

Samson *was mocked by the Philistines - It so happened when they were in high spirits, that they said, "Call for Samson, that he may amuse us." So they called for Samson from the prison, and he entertained them. And they made him stand between the pillars. (Judges 16:25-note)*

*The supreme example is that of sinful men mocking the God-Man Christ Jesus "and will hand Him over to the Gentiles to **mock** and **scourge** and **crucify** Him, and on the third day He will be raised up (Matthew 20:19).*

PERSONAL QUESTIONS

Have you ever been mocked for being a follower of Christ?

_____
_____
_____
_____
_____

Would you walk away from your faith in Christ if you were being mocked?

_____
_____
_____
_____

Please pray for students who are in schools where they are being mocked and insulted for believing God's Word.

DAY 37 - Heb. 11:37

Amplified: *They were stoned to death; they were lured with tempting offers [to renounce their faith]; they were sawn asunder; they were slaughtered by the sword; [while they were alive] they had to go about wrapped in the skins of sheep and goats, utterly destitute, oppressed, cruelly treated— (Amplified Bible - Lockman)*

KJV: *They were stoned, they were sawn asunder, were tempted, were slain with the sword: they wandered about in sheepskins and goatskins; being destitute, afflicted, tormented;*

NLT: *Some died by stoning, and some were sawed in half; others were killed with the sword. Some went about in skins of sheep and goats, hungry and oppressed and mistreated. (NLT - Tyndale House)*

Phillips: *They were killed by stoning, by being sawn in two; they were tempted by specious promises of release and then were killed with the sword. Many became refugees with nothing but sheepskins or goatskins to cover them. They lost everything and yet were spurned and ill-treated (Phillips: Touchstone)*

"SAWN USUNDER?"

Henry Morris - *According to Jewish tradition, the prophet Isaiah was executed by being sawn in two during the reign of the evil son of King Hezekiah, Manasseh.* (**Defender's Study Bible**)

HOW ISAIAH DIED

Lane *records that according to "mutually complementary rabbinic sources, Manasseh, enraged because Isaiah had prophesied the destruction of the Temple, ordered his arrest. Isaiah fled to the hill country and hid in the trunk of a cedar tree. He was discovered when the king ordered the tree cut down. Isaiah was tortured with a saw because he had taken refuge in the trunk of a tree. (Lane, W. L. Vol. 47B: Word Biblical Commentary: Hebrews 9-13. Word Biblical Commentary (390). Dallas: Word, Incorporated)*

"SOME WERE STONED"

We can fast forward to the New Testament and think of a great man of faith who was stoned to death for sharing the Gospel of Jesus Christ. His name was Stephen.

Acts 7:54-60

When the members of the Sanhedrin heard this, they were furious and gnashed their teeth at him. [55] *But Stephen, full of the Holy Spirit, looked up to heaven and saw the glory of God, and Jesus standing at the right hand of God.*

56 "Look," he said, "I see heaven open and the Son of Man standing at the right hand of God." 57 At this they covered their ears and, yelling at the top of their voices, they all rushed at him, 58 dragged him out of the city and began to stone him. Meanwhile, the witnesses laid their coats at the feet of a young man named Saul.

59 While they were stoning him, Stephen prayed, "Lord Jesus, receive my spirit." 60 Then he fell on his knees and cried out, "Lord, do not hold this sin against them." When he had said this, he fell asleep.

PERSONAL QUESTIONS

Why would God allow this to happen to Stephen? He was faithfully preaching the Gospel and was killed. Why?

_____
_____
_____

Look at Acts 8:1 to find one of the answers to this question. Do you know how that man is in verse one?

_____
_____

Lord, be glorified by my life……or by my death.

DAY 38 – Heb. 11:38

Phillips: *by a world that was too evil to see their worth. They lived as vagrants in the desert, on the mountains, or in caves or holes in the ground. (Phillips: Touchstone)*

Wuest: *men of whom the world was not worthy, wandering over deserts and mountains, and in caves and holes of the earth. (Eerdmans)*

Young's Literal: *of whom the world was not worthy; in deserts wandering, and in mountains, and in caves, and in the holes of the earth;*

THE WORLD WAS NOT WORTHY.

"Men of whom the world was not worthy" – *W.E. Vine comments that "The statement expresses the divine estimate. The world counts those who are true witnesses to God not worthy of itself. God reverses the comparison. Separation from the world and its ways always brings its contempt. The world will one day be compelled to acknowledge that God is right. Phillips paraphrases it "by a world that was too evil to see their worth."*

AM I WALKING WORTHY?

"Am I conducting myself in a manner worthy of the Gospel?" is a good question for us to ask ourselves regularly.

THINK ABOUT THIS!

*Right thinking should always lead to right conduct. Knowledge and obedience go together. One cannot separate **learning** from **living**. The idea of "worthy" is that the conduct of the saints weigh as much as the character of Christ. Why? Because when we are surrendered to His will, He is living His life through us via His indwelling Spirit. Ultimately His conduct is the only conduct which is truly worthy, for no other conduct would balance God's perfect scales. Christ alone pleases the Father completely and as we allow Christ to rule and reign in our lives, our lives become pleasing to the Father.*

SUMMARY OF THIS SECTION

Let me sum up this section of Hebrews chapter 11 with four applications.

(1) Faith is ready to sacrifice present comfort for future reward with Christ. *Faith recognizes that this life is very short in comparison with eternity. With Paul, faith recognizes that "momentary, light affliction is producing for us an eternal weight of glory far beyond all comparison" (2Co 4:17). In Paul's case, this "light affliction" included beatings, imprisonments, being stoned, shipwrecked, and often being in danger of death (2Co 11:23, 24, 25, 26, 27)! When you experience "light affliction," do you grumble or do you joyfully trust God?*

(2) Faith lives with a God-ward focus, not with a focus on people or things. *The saints mentioned in our text could endure mockings, scourgings, imprisonments, and death because their focus was on God, not on other people or things. They were looking to eternity, not to this vapor of life here. Calvin put it this way, "we ought to live only so as to live to God: as soon as we are not permitted to live to God, we ought willingly and not reluctantly to meet death."*

(3) Faith trusts and obeys God, leaving the results to His sovereignty. *Some trust and obey God and He grants spectacular results. Others trust and obey the same mighty God and He enables them to endure horrific trials in His strength. The difference is not in the people or in their faith, but in God's sovereign purpose in each situation. We know the same God that these Old Testament saints knew, and we have even more, in that we know Christ personally. So we should trust Him as they did, whether He chooses to put us to death, as He did with the apostle James, or to deliver us from death for a while, as He did with Peter.*

(4) Faithfulness to Jesus Christ counts more than anything else, even than life itself.

As Martin Luther put it in his words to the classic hymn of the ages - "A Mighty Fortress"

*Let goods and kindred go,
this mortal life also;*

*the body they may kill:
God's truth abideth still;
His kingdom is forever.*

Trust God in whatever difficult situations you face. One day soon you will hear, "Well done, good and faithful slave.... Enter into the joy of your master" (Mt 24:21)

PERSONAL QUESTIONS

Why is it wrong to judge whether we have God's blessing by the visible results?

_____
_____
_____
_____
_____
_____

Which believer in Christ have you seen who most walked worthy of the Lord and made a deep impact on you faith?

_____
_____
_____
_____

"FAITH IS NOT THE BELIEF THAT GOD WILL DO WHAT YOU WANT. IT IS THE BELIEF THAT GOD WILL DO WHAT IS RIGHT."

MAX LUCADO

quoteseverlasting.com

DAY 39 – Heb. 11:39

Amplified: *And all of these, though they won divine approval by [means of] their faith, did not receive the fulfillment of what was promised, (Amplified Bible - Lockman)*

KJV: *And these all, having obtained a good report through faith, received not the promise:*

NLT: *All of these people we have mentioned received God's approval because of their faith, yet none of them received all that God had promised. (NLT - Tyndale House)*

Phillips: *All these won a glowing testimony to their faith, but they did not then and there receive the fulfilment of the promise. (Phillips: Touchstone)*

Wuest: *And these all, although they had witness borne to them through their faith, did not receive the promise. (Eerdmans)*

Young's Literal: *and these all, having been testified to through the faith, did not receive the promise.*

WORD STUDY

"Having gained approval" *(martureo from mártus = witness, one who has information or knowledge of something & hence can bring to light or confirm something; English ~ martyr)) means to be a witness, to testify, to give evidence, to give testimony, to affirm that one has seen or heard or experienced something. To be well reported. It means to provide* information about a person or an event concerning which the speaker has direct knowledge.

Martureo in some context is used in the sense of making an important and solemn declaration. It can be used in the sense of confirmation or approval and so to affirm n a supportive manner.

Martureo is another key word in Hebrews, with almost 10% of the NT uses of this key word.

Hebrews 7:8 (note) - In this case mortal men receive tithes, but in that case one receives them, of whom it **is witnessed** that he lives on.

Hebrews 10:15 (note) - And the Holy Spirit also **testifies** to us; for after saying,

Hebrews 11:2 (note) - For by it the men of old **gained approval**.

Hebrews 11:4 (note) - By faith Abel offered to God a better sacrifice than Cain, through which he **obtained the testimony** that he was righteous, God **testifying** about his gifts, and through faith, though he is dead, he still speaks.

Hebrews 11:5 (note) - By faith Enoch was taken up so that he would not see death; AND HE WAS NOT FOUND BECAUSE GOD TOOK HIM UP; for he **obtained the witness** that before his being taken up he was pleasing to God.

Hebrews 11:39 (note) - And all these, **having gained approval** through their faith, did not receive what was promised

WHAT HAPPENED TO THE FAITHFUL?

Now, what was the result for those who were faithful in persecution, deprivation, and death?

First, they "were all commended for their faith" (v39a). *This is the way the chapter began—"Now faith is being sure of what we hope for and certain of what we do not see. This is what the ancients were commended for" (v1, v2)—and this is how it ends. All the faithful (the known and unknown, the famously triumphant and those who anonymously persevered in suffering) were "commended for their faith." God forgets no one who loves and serves him! It is his great pleasure to commend faith!*

The second result is that "none"—that is, none of the great triumphant members of the Hall of Faith or those who persevered without earthly triumphs—"none of them received what had been promised" (v39b). *Although many promises had been given and fulfilled in their lifetimes, they did not receive the great promise—namely, the coming of the Messiah and salvation in Him. Every one of the faithful in Old Testament times died before Jesus appeared. They entered Heaven with the promise unfulfilled.*

Why is this? The answer is given in our final verse: "God had planned something better for us so that only together with us would they be made perfect" (v40). No one was "made perfect" under the Old Covenant, because Christ had not yet died. They were saved, but not until Jesus' work on the cross was complete could salvation be perfect. **Their salvation looked ahead to what Christ would do. Ours looks back to what he has done—and ours is "more" perfect now but someday in glory totally perfect.**

PERSONAL QUESTIONS

Has God ever left you hanging when you prayed for Him to deliver you?

_____
_____
_____

If yes, how did that make you feel about God's faithfulness?

_____
_____
_____
_____

Looking back now, can you see how God used this hurtful experience in your life to build your faith?

_____
_____
_____
_____

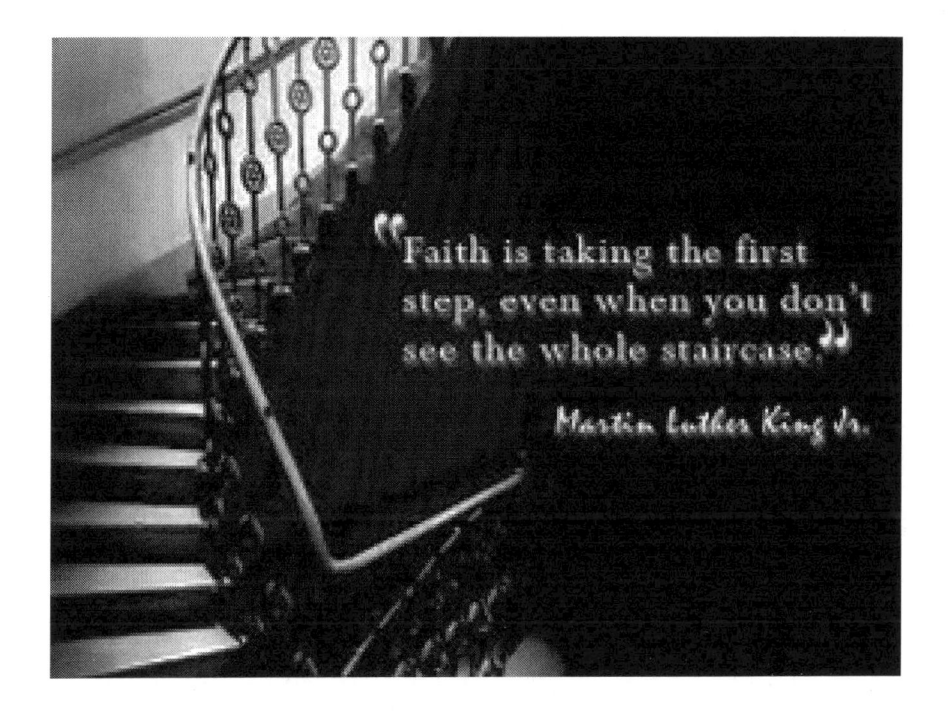

> "Faith is taking the first step, even when you don't see the whole staircase."
>
> — Martin Luther King Jr.

DAY 40 – Heb. 11:40

Amplified: Because God had us in mind and had something better and greater in view for us, so that they [these heroes and heroines of faith] should not come to perfection apart from us [before we could join them]. (*Amplified Bible - Lockman*)

KJV: God having provided some better thing for us, that they without us should not be made perfect.

NET: For God had provided something better for us, so that they would be made perfect together with us.

NLT: For God had far better things in mind for us that would also benefit them, for they can't receive the prize at the end of the race until we finish the race. (*NLT - Tyndale House*)

Phillips: God had something better planned for our day, and it was not his plan that they should reach perfection without us. (*Phillips: Touchstone*)

Wuest: God having provided some better thing for us, in order that they without us should not be brought to completeness. (*Eerdmans*)

Young's Literal: God for us something better having provided, that apart from us they might not be made perfect.

WHAT HAPPENED TO THE O.T. SAINTS??

"Something better for us" - *This phrase denotes the reality we as NT believers have found in Christ, which the men and women of faith in the OT would attain only after their earthly life ended. We are already recipients of the blessings of the new covenant in His blood.*

They would not fully know these blessings until the resurrection of Christ, who at the time between His death on the Cross and His resurrection set free a host of captives of OT saints from Abraham's bosom so that they are now present with Him in heaven, awaiting the establishment of His kingdom for His 1000 year reign at the beginning of which they will receive their resurrected bodies.

<u>**Matthew 27:51-54**</u> *[51]At that moment the curtain of the temple was torn in two from top to bottom. The earth shook, the rocks split [52]and the tombs broke open. The bodies of many holy people who had died were raised to life. [53]They came out of the tombs after Jesus' resurrection and went into the holy city and appeared to many people.*

How great is our advantage! Right now, we live in the so much better New Covenant. We now have a high priest who has offered a perfect sacrifice for our sins once and for all. Our Savior/Priest sits at the right hand of the Father and prays for us. We have a better hope!

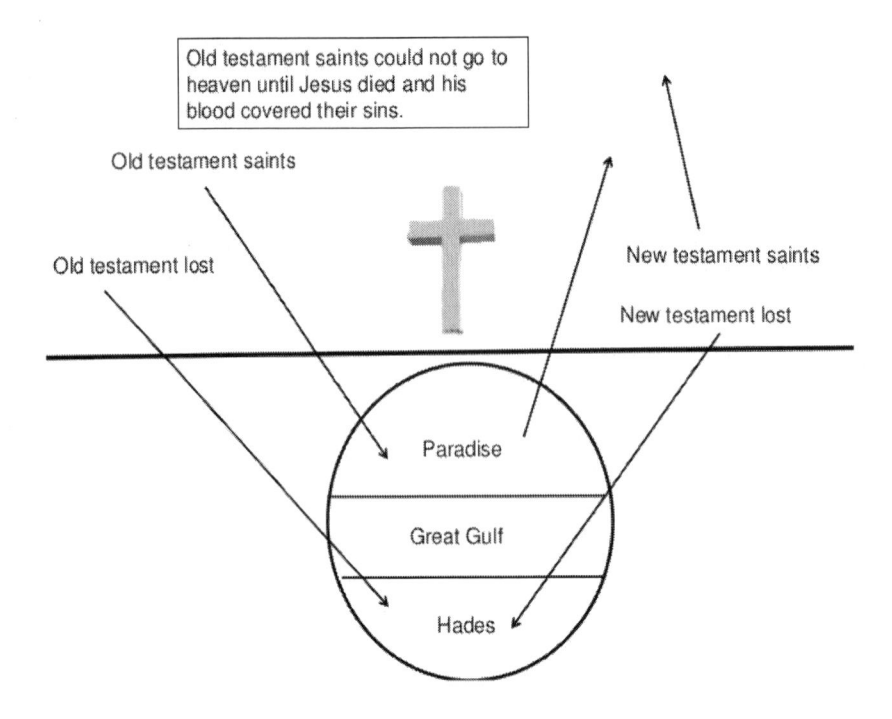

No one could enter into Heaven until Jesus came and paid the price for redemption. Now, He is the Way, the Truth and the Life and no one comes to the Father in Heaven except through Jesus Christ.

MY FINAL QUESTION.
Do you have a personal relationship with Jesus Christ? Have you invited Him to be your Lord and Savior? If not, take the greatest journey of faith of all and meet Jesus!

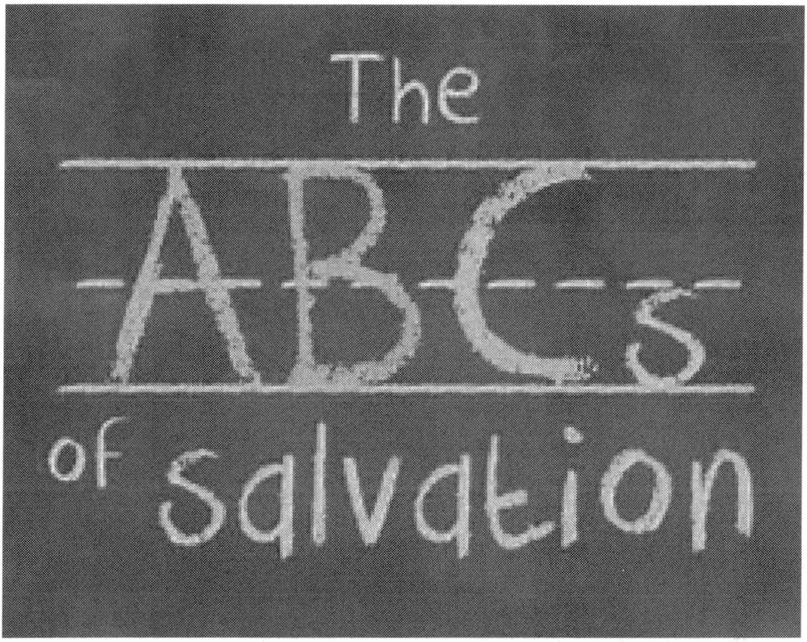
The
ABCs
of salvation

HOW TO TRUST CHRIST AS YOUR SAVIOR

God is a perfect Creator and Heaven is a perfect place. Unfortunately, that leaves you and me with a problem because we have all sinned and come short of the perfection of God (Romans 3:23).

However, God loves us and does not want us to spend eternity away from Him (II Peter 3:9). The reason Hell was created was for Satan and his angels who rebelled (Matthew 25:41).

You don't have to go to Heaven – God is a gentleman. You have a choice. But He has paid the price for your sin and made a way possible for you to go to Heaven through His perfect Son, Jesus Christ (John 14:6).

The way to Heaven is not through good works.
The way to Heaven is not through joining a church.
The way to Heaven is not through anything we can do.
The way to Heaven is through a personal relationship with Jesus Christ.

How do you invite Christ into your life? It's as easy as A-B-C!

- ***ASK** Jesus into your life right now. ("Whoever calls on the Name of the Lord shall be saved" - Romans 10:13).*

- ***BELIEVE that Jesus paid for your sin*** *and rose from the dead to prove He is God. ("Believe on the Lord Jesus Christ and you will be saved" - Acts 16:31).*

- ***CLAIM your forgiveness*** *based upon the facts of His Word, not your feelings. ("These things have I written unto you that believe on the name of the Son of God; that ye may know that ye have eternal life, and that ye may believe on the name of the Son of God" - I John 5:13).*

Prayer To Trust Christ As Savior

Lord Jesus, I invite you into my life right now. Take away all of my sin. Give me a home in Heaven. Make a brand new person and give me the power to live right according to Your Word. I thank you for hearing my prayer today. I give you the reigns to my life and I commit myself to You. Amen.

What Do I Do Now?

*G- **Go to Church and worship** regularly. Find a Bible-believing church which loves Jesus and loves people.*

*R- **Read the Word of God daily.** Start by reading the Gospel of John. Get a Bible and download a Bible version app (such as You Version) to your cell phone.*

*O- **Obey God's Word.** It is your final authority in life. The first step of obedience is to follow the Lord in baptism in a church where there is a family of believers in Jesus Christ.*

*W – **Witness to others** and tell them what Jesus has done for you.*

APPENDIX

PERSONAL QUESTION

What did God say to you from Hebrews chapter 11 about your faith and life?

Write it down on the next page.

*What changes are you going to make
in your life as a result of understanding
Hebrews 11?*

SERMON NOTES & JOURNALING

Thank You

*Thanks for taking the
Journey with Jesus
& me.*

Larry Petton

Made in the USA
Lexington, KY
08 September 2017